MARRIAGE FOR GOD'S SAKE

MARRIAGE
for
GOD'S SAKE
A Guide for Catholics

BY
REV. THOMAS G. MORROW

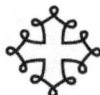

Angelico Press

For information, address:
Angelico Press, Ltd.
169 Monitor St.
Brooklyn, NY 11222
www.angelicopress.com

ppr 979-8-89280-095-2
cloth 979-8-89280-096-9
ebook 979-8-89280-097-6

Book and cover design
by Michael Schrauzer

TABLE OF CONTENTS

ACKNOWLEDGMENTS

My sincere thanks to Barbara Meng and Olga Fairfax who so carefully proofread this manuscript and recommended corrections.

CHAPTER 1

Commit!

T HEY HAD THEIR HEALTH, SIX-FIGURE salaries, a beautiful house, two cars, two great kids, and a vasectomy. And they were miserable. Julie and Greg were married in 1987 and had their first child, Christopher, in 1988. In 1989 they gave birth to Lauren. The doctors told them they were the "perfect family" with two children, one boy, one girl. So, Greg had a vasectomy. They were church-going Catholics, but didn't truly know the Church's teachings on marriage.

After several months of staying at home with the children, Julie began to feel empty and restless. This, coupled with the pressure of friends, drove her to take a job outside the home. They didn't need the money, but she needed to be "fulfilled." Her self-worth seemed to come from her job and the money she made.

Little by little their relationship and family as a whole began to suffer. Careers became the most important thing in their lives—especially for Julie. They were still going to Mass every Sunday but it was more out of habit than anything else. Needless to say, God was not at the center of their lives. They prayed only in times of need or when things weren't going right. Then they would ask, "God, why is our life like this?"

Working and making money were far more important to them than spending time together as a family. They even stopped having family dinners. Fast food was a common meal for the kids because there was no time to cook.

They allowed money and material things to become their god. They sacrificed anything and everything to achieve it. Their lives were inundated with networking, happy hours, and any event where they could meet and rub elbows with those who had attained the wealth they were seeking.

After about a year or so Greg began to see that all of this "stuff" was not that important. But Julie wasn't there yet. She began to believe that Greg was not the same person she married because they no longer shared the same goals. Not surprisingly, they began to grow apart.

They started finding ways to fill their days so they wouldn't have to be together. Julie became a gym rat and worked out as much as she could. Greg hung out with his buddies, and they, in a sense, became his family.

For four years they maintained this lifestyle. They started buying more things to fill the void in their relationship. When having more and more failed them, they tried to find happiness in other ways, and eventually in other people. They were clueless about what was missing in their lives.

In 1997 Julie was offered a job in San Antonio, over an hour from home, to work in sales for an independent yellow page company. She took the job, and started coming home only one night a week and on the weekends. The money she was making was so good that it became the excuse for continuing to work out of town.

Eventually, those feelings of not wanting to live without the other became thoughts of how to avoid each other, and Julie's new job made it very easy. They grew far apart and their sexual life became a selfish act of pleasure, not a self-surrender in love. Things got so bad that thoughts of infidelity crept in, followed by unfaithful acts. Sex between the two no longer had meaning or feelings attached.

Not only were they growing apart from each other but they were growing further away from God as well. Eventually things got so bad that Greg suggested the unimaginable: divorce. Greg reached the point where he felt that he couldn't take it any longer. Julie agreed, so it seemed like a done deal. They would get a divorce.

They went to see their priest and tell him about their decision. To illustrate how ignorant they were, they were hoping to win his support. They made an appointment and went in to tell him their plans. He sat there quietly as they tried to justify their actions, and when they were finished, he asked them a series of questions: "What is God's intention for the marriage covenant? What does the Church teach? What are some of the writings of St. Paul on marriage?" Julie and Greg looked at each other, shrugged their shoulders and replied with a big "I don't know." All they knew was they were Catholic, got baptized and confirmed, fell in love and got married, and now they felt they couldn't live this way anymore.

Their priest then suggested that they go home and do some studying and praying before they made this decision final. Even though they felt that they could not go on in this relationship, something inside them said, "Let's give it a try."

By this time, they had talked to other priests, been to counseling, and tried everything else you can imagine. But they never thought of Scripture, or even the teachings of the Church for that matter, nor had they even thought about praying for their marriage. So, they went home to do their research.

Like most Catholics, Greg not only had to find their Bible but also had to dust it off before he could begin to read. He started with the writings of St. Paul. Then he went to the writings of some of the early Church Fathers and on to various encyclicals, in particular John Paul II's exhortation, *The Role of the Christian Family*,[1] and the grace of God literally began to descend upon him. You could say that the scales fell from his eyes and he began to see their situation and life itself through God's eyes for the first time.

Greg went to Julie and said, "What were we thinking? This is not at all what God intended marriage to be like." They immediately went to God and prayed the following: "God, we're tired of trying to live our lives as society says we should, and we're tired of trying things our way. It just hasn't worked. So, we ask you to come into our lives and show us how you want us to live our marriage." Greg went even further, saying that if he delivered them from this mess, they would dedicate the rest of their lives to working in marriage and family ministry.

To some this account may sound a bit weird, but it's true, and anyone who has had an experience like theirs knows exactly what they were talking about. Well, you've heard the saying "Be careful what you pray for . . ." From that day, amazing things began to happen. Every day became a new journey for them. They had no idea what a jewel they had in their Catholic faith. They began to overflow with an excitement that they had never felt before.

They mutually made the decision to quit their jobs because they knew that not only were they taking them away from each other but they were taking them

---

[1] Or *Familiaris Consortio*.

away from their children and God as well. They felt that they had found out where they had gone wrong and anything that would interfere with their marriage had to go. They made God number one, each other second, the kids third, family and friends next, and everything else wherever they fell.

As they began to strengthen their relationship with God, their marriage relationship began to get stronger. They fixed their relationship with God and began to celebrate this sacrament the way he intended, and the graces flowed. This is why marriage is considered to be one of the great mysteries.

There is more to their story, but we'll save that for later. Greg and Julie saved their marriage, and many more blessings followed (more on those blessings later on herein). And, of course, they were happy. They traded in their miserable, empty marriage for a marriage according to God's plan and they were so glad they did. Today, they have a ministry for married couples, The Alexander House.[2]

Julie and Greg would have been delighted had the priest told them, "Oh sure, you can get a divorce if you want. Then you can seek an annulment." And they would have become another of the thousands of people who end their marriage without having tried, to save it with every fiber of their being.

This is not what God intended. Jesus spoke about marriage as follows: "What God has joined together, let no one separate" (Mt 19:6). He also said, "Anyone who divorces his wife and marries another commits adultery, and whoever marries a woman divorced from her husband commits adultery" (Lk 16:18).

---

[2] www.thealexanderhouse.org/.

Why is the divorce/separation rate in the US over 40 percent?[3] Perhaps one reason is that many seem unaware of what a large undertaking marriage is. Marriage vows are a big responsibility. But if lived out to the full in the Lord, they bring great happiness.

It is an amazing thing in this day of trivialization of promises and vows, to say to another person, "I, John, take you, Mary, to be my wife. I promise to be true to you in good times and bad, in sickness and health. I will love you and honor you all the days of my life."

What an awesome promise, what an awesome relationship is marriage. Think about that long and hard. *I will be true to you in good times and bad.* That means I will be faithful to you, my wife, when things are not going well between us. I will be faithful to you, my husband, when you're out of a job, when there's no money, when you come home late. I will be there for you when you gain weight, when you turn gray, when you become bald, when your beauty fades.

Marriage is not about maximizing pleasure, but about following a call from God to love this person selflessly and to raise up saints together. It's not about drawing all the joy and delight you can from your emotional love together, but about *building a serene, quiet, enduring friendship through kindness, graciousness, and generous self-giving, even when it hurts; and spending yourselves together nurturing godly children.* And, of course, through this, helping each other to grow in holiness.

---

[3] "Almost 50 percent of all marriages in the United States will end in divorce or separation. Researchers estimate that 41 percent of all first marriages end in divorce. 60 percent of second marriages end in divorce. 73 percent of all third marriages end in divorce." Wilkinson & Finkbeiner, LLP, "Divorce Statistics: Over 115 Studies, Facts and Rates for 2024," https://www.wf-lawyers.com/divorce-statistics-and-facts/. See also https://www.fatherly.com/love-money/what-is-divorce-rate-america/.

MARRIAGE VOWS

I will be true to you in sickness and in health. That means I will be faithful to you even if you get MS, or cancer, or some other serious disease and are bed-ridden. I will be there when you get old, when you use a walker, when you are in a wheelchair. I will be there for you.

I will love you and honor you all the days of my life. In other words, I will work for your good and your happiness every day, no matter what happens, no matter how unkind you were to me last night, no matter how hurt I feel. I will still work for your good.

And, not only will I love you, I will *honor* you as well. That means I will respect you; I will uphold your dignity; I will not treat you lightly or as an inferior. I will hold you up as someone special, someone precious to me. And I'll do this every day of my life. (More on honoring in a moment.)

Whew! That's a vow you make before God, before his altar. In other words, it would be one thing to promise this to your spouse, but a vow is calling God to witness this so that if you fail to keep it, it's far more serious than just breaking a promise or a contract. This is serious business! You gave your word . . . to your spouse before *God*. What is your word worth? Are you one who sticks by your word, or one who gives it lightly, without much thought? Remember, you gave this word before God.

HONOR YOUR SPOUSE

When you marry, you promised to *honor* your spouse. That means you will always respect him/her, you will always uphold his/her dignity as a human person. You will do this, not because he/she deserves it, but because you vowed to do it at God's altar.

How do you do this? You resolve now, long before your wedding, to always be polite to your spouse, to try to say "please" and "thank you" consistently, or ". . . if you would be so kind."

"Oh, Father, that sounds so formal. I couldn't do that. And I could never remember every time anyway." Formal or not, the couples who do this are extremely successful in their marriages. I've seen it in action, and it's a joy to be with these couples. And, as for remembering it, once you make it a habit, you don't have to think about it anymore. It takes several weeks, perhaps even months, to make this language a habit, but once you do, if you don't slip back, you'll have a marital treasure. Hang on to it for dear life. It will work wonders in your marriage.

One woman called me when her husband moved out. One of the things she told me was that he had come home one day with some very expensive shoes—two pairs! "Do you know what I did with them, Father? I threw them at him."

"Where'd you learn to do that?" I asked her. "Did your mother do that?"

"No."

"Well, Christian women don't do things like that. Please, don't ever do that again."

She didn't. After lots more discussion they were back together and I urged them to work at *honoring* each other every day. They promised to do that when they got married, after all. They did, and it worked.

Remember every day to honor your spouse. You promised.

A GOOD COURTSHIP

The first step in making the lifelong commitment of marriage is to spend a good long time in courtship to see if this is really the commitment you want to make and if this is the person you want to make it with. However, if you are reading this, you are probably already married, and so the issue of courtship length is a moot point.

Nonetheless, if you already are married, you still may have the chance in the future to encourage another couple—or perhaps several—to prepare well for marriage. Please, please tell them to take their time in courtship. Marriage is a HUGE commitment.

FIREPROOF YOUR MARRIAGE

Some years ago a woman came to me to talk about her marriage. She said, "When our five children are old enough I am going to divorce my husband." (The youngest was six, so I guess she was planning to hang on for at least ten years.)

I told her, "Before you do that, I want you to see this movie." I handed her the DVD *Fireproof*. I also gave her the book *The Love Dare*, which is the blueprint the husband used in *Fireproof* to save his marriage. "I want you to promise me that you will do everything in your power to be kind and loving to your husband, because that's what you promised to do on your wedding day . . . and, of course, because you're a Christian."

She agreed.

I should explain briefly that the movie *Fireproof* is about a couple whose marriage is on the rocks. The husband complains to his father that divorce is almost inevitable. The father gives him a little diary (*The Love Dare*) and asks him to spend forty days doing the things he has written in it to try to reignite his relationship with his wife. The son reluctantly agrees. At first his romantic overtures are rudely rebuffed, and the son is often on the phone telling his father it's not working.

Nonetheless, the father encourages him to continue for the remaining days, and the son agrees . . . barely.

Of course, by the end of this (award winning) movie, the wife warms up to the husband and there is a reconciliation. Along the way, the son acquires newfound faith in God.

I gave it to that wife, as I have given it to many other spouses in troubled marriages, to show her that when all seems hopeless in a marriage, there is still hope. And to show her that the love vowed by a couple on their wedding day is something they *will*, not something they *feel*. It is something they will to do, not something that automatically wells up within them.

In any event, the wife took home the DVD and book and began to work on it. Her five daughters watched the movie with her and they were fascinated at the prospect of her project. They encouraged her and kept checking on how things were going.

I warned the wife it would probably be several months before she would see any results, so she should be patient. In several months she *did* see some results. The husband began to warm up, and be more grateful to have a wife and five children in his life. The change was remarkable.

I recommend the movie *Fireproof* and its companion *The Love Dare* to every married couple, to every family. It is one of the best things I have ever seen for troubled marriages. But even if your marriage is wonderful, this is a great movie to see because of its many fine messages about marriage.

MARRIAGE SAVERS

There is another reason why everyone should see *Fireproof*: we Christians are all called to be "marriage savers."

In other words, as Pastor Michael J. McManus explains in his book, *Marriage Savers*, we have an obligation to help our friends and acquaintances to live out their marriage vows. When a friend comes to you and tells you how difficult his marriage is, you shouldn't respond, "Maybe it's time for a divorce," regardless of how you feel.

So often when couples tell me their marital troubles, I say to myself, "This seems hopeless." When they finish, I invariably say to them, "There is hope for your marriage. I have seen worse marriages survive" (which I have). Marriage is an amazing institution, filled with tremendous potential. I have seen *miracles* happen in so many bad marriages, even when just one spouse sets out to save the marriage.

That is why I would virtually never recommend that a couple throw in the towel on their miserable marriage. And I hope anyone reading this will take the same approach, doing everything in their power to make their marriage work.

THE BEST MARRIAGE SAVER EVER

There is one thing that saves marriages more than any other thing. Those who do it have a divorce rate of one out of 1,152. What is it? Praying together daily.[4] For some hearing this it may seem intimidating. Could Lisa and I really pray together... *daily*? It seems so radical, so different.[5]

---

[4] Lavern Nissley, "An Amazing Secret to Marriage Success," Encompass Connection Center, March 26, 2019, https://www.encompasscc.org/blog/an-amazing-secret-to-marriage-success. A 1997 Gallup Poll done by the National Association of Marriage Enhancement showed the divorce rate among couples who regularly pray together (in addition to grace before meals) is one out of 1,152.

[5] When I was dating—long before I entered the seminary or had an inkling that I might have a priestly vocation—I suggested to my solidly Catholic girlfriend that we pray together sometime.

But when it comes to making a marriage last, a couple should be very radical. What in this world could be more important, after our faith in God?

Another study published in the *Journal of Marriage and Family* found similar results for couples pursuing faith activities together.[6] Marriage writer Lavern Nissley reports,

> Even *Redbook*, in an article [Lavern's wife] Ronda read, had this to say from a University of Chicago survey: "75 percent of the Americans who pray with their spouses reported that their marriages are 'very happy' (compared to 57 percent of those who don't). Those who pray together are also more likely to say they respect each other, discuss their marriage together, and—stop the presses—rate their spouses as skilled lovers." Well there you go![7]

Nissley goes on to say,

> The marriage workshop we attended in March, 1990 inspired Ronda and me to begin praying together daily. It changed our lives and likely saved our marriage. No, it didn't remove all conflicts and frustrations we have with each other. But it has helped us navigate a whole host of varied challenges through the years following. Not sure where we would be without that daily habit of praying together.[8]

She asked, "Out loud?" as if she had never heard of such a thing. It took her a while to warm up to the idea!

[6] Christopher G. Ellison, Amy M. Burdette, and W. Bradford Wilcox, "The Couple That Prays Together: Race and Ethnicity, Religion, and Relationship Quality Among Working-Age Adults," *Journal of Marriage and Family* 72 (August 2010): 963–75.

[7] Lavern Nissley, "An Amazing Secret to Marriage Success," Encompass Connection Center, March 26, 2019, https://www.encompasscc.org/blog/an-amazing-secret-to-marriage-success.

[8] Ibid.

Couples praying together is all about intimacy, and (personal) intimacy is at the heart of a good marriage. Few couples pray together daily and reach a deep intimacy in their marriage, but those who have reached it find it profoundly enriching and delightful.

What would be a good prayer to pray together? I recommend the rosary. Why? First of all, Blessed Mary asked at Fatima for five mysteries of the rosary daily for world peace, and today it seems that we should pray for world peace more than ever. Secondly, among those Catholics who pray more than ten minutes a day, I would estimate that 80 percent pray the rosary. And, when prayed correctly, the rosary is a deeply meditative prayer, based on the life of Christ and his Church.[9]

Some more reasons: Pope St. John Paul II called the rosary his "favorite prayer." St. Francis de Sales said, "The best method of praying is to pray the rosary." And Archbishop Fulton Sheen wrote,

> The rosary is the meeting ground of the uneducated and the learned; the place where simple love grows in knowledge and where the knowing mind grows in love…
>
> The rosary is the book of the blind, where they see, and there enact the greatest drama of love the world has ever known; it is the book of the simple which initiates them into mysteries and knowledge more satisfying than the education of other men; it is the book of the aged, whose eyes close on the shadow of this world, and open on the substance of the next. The power of the rosary is beyond description.[10]

---

[9] I have written a booklet on the rosary with poetry and meditations for each mystery, "World's Most Powerful Mysteries." You may download the text at https://cfalive.com/collections/booklets/products/worlds-most-powerful-mysteries.

[10] Fulton J. Sheen, *The World's First Love* (New York: McGraw-Hill, 1952), 188–89.

If you do pray the rosary[11] together I recommend also spending two or three minutes three or four times a week in spontaneous prayer for your intentions, your gratitude, and your sorrow for your failings. This will make your prayer more personal.[12]

Keep in mind that attending daily Mass is the greatest source of grace, and for a couple to do that is a wonderful practice, but that does not preclude the rosary or some spontaneous prayer together.

What if occasionally you can't pray together? Pray the rosary separately (world peace is still a worthy reason!) and try to spend a couple of minutes together in spontaneous prayer.

It's a good idea to avoid spending too much time for your prayer together at first. Otherwise you may find yourselves skipping it due to lack of time.

Oh, and whenever things are difficult, be sure to ask God together for the grace of your sacrament. It is a powerful grace.

> Christian partners are therefore strengthened, and as it were consecrated, by a special sacrament for the duties and the dignity of their state. By the power of this sacrament they fulfill their obligations to each other and to their family and are filled with the spirit of

---

[11] To avoid making the rosary a rote prayer, use different booklets, leaflets, etc. containing meditations, or pull up YouTube and search "visual rosary joyful [or sorrowful/glorious/luminous] mysteries" and you will see several options that offer accompanying artwork (or videos) for each mystery.

[12] For example, the husband might pray this: "I give you thanks, O Lord, for my wonderful family, for my wife especially, for my health, and for my job. Please help me to be more kind with my sweet wife..." For several ideas on different prayers couples can pray together, see Fr. Michael Denk's "Catholic Prayer for Marriage: Couples That Pray Together Stay Together," 2019, https://blog.theprodigalfather.org/catholic-prayer-for-marriage.

Christ. This spirit pervades their whole lives with faith, hope and love. Thus they promote their own perfection and each other's sanctification, and so contribute together to the greater glory of God.[13]

The state of marriage is one that requires more virtue and constancy than any other. It is a perpetual exercise of mortification.... You must then dispose yourself to it with a particular care, that from this thyme plant, in spite of the bitter nature of its juice, you may be able to draw and make the honey of a holy life.[14]

---

[13] *Gaudium et Spes*, n. 48.
[14] St. Francis de Sales, *Thy Will Be Done, Letters to Persons in the World* (Manchester, NH: Sophia Institute Press, 1995), 42.

CHAPTER II

Why Not Divorce?

> ...The LORD is witness between you and the wife of your youth, with whom you have broken faith though she is your companion, your betrothed wife. Did he not make one being, with flesh and spirit: and what does that one require but godly offspring? You must then safeguard life that is your own, and not break faith with the wife of your youth. For I hate divorce, says the LORD, the God of Israel... (Malachi 2:14–16)

What did Jesus say about divorce?

> Some Pharisees came, and to test him they asked, "Is it lawful for a man to divorce his wife?" He answered them, "What did Moses command you?" They said, "Moses allowed a man to write a certificate of dismissal and to divorce her." But Jesus said to them, "Because of your hardness of heart he wrote this commandment for you. But from the beginning of creation, 'God made them male and female.' 'For this reason a man shall leave his father and mother and be joined to his wife, and the two shall become one flesh.' So they are no longer two, but one flesh. Therefore what God has joined together, let no one separate."
>
> Then in the house the disciples asked him again about this matter. He said to them, "Whoever divorces his wife and marries another commits adultery against her; and if she divorces her husband and

marries another, she commits adultery."
(Mk 10:2–12)[1]

COUPLES WHO DIDN'T DIVORCE

In addition to God's disdain for divorce, it would seem to be worthwhile to consider the experiences of couples who have struggled in their marriages. Did divorce make them happier than those who stayed with their marriages? And how did those who stayed survive? In 2002, the Institute for American Values published a study titled, "Does Divorce Make People Happy?"[2]

The authors looked at data from the National Survey of Families and Households (NSFH), in which couples indicated their marital happiness and overall happiness in the late 1980s, and then again five years later. *Of spouses unhappily married but who stayed married, 64 percent indicated they were happy in their marriage five years later!* The unhappier the marriage, the greater the improvement: Among those who described their marriage as "life in hell," 78 percent indicated they were happy five years later when they stayed in their marriage. Of those who separated or divorced, just 53 percent said they were happy.[3] "With the important

---

[1] The prohibition against divorce is equally firm in Luke 16:18. In Matthew 5:31–32 there is an exception clause, "except in the case of *porneia*," which was in the past translated from Greek as "unchastity" or "adultery." More recent scholarship has put forth convincing arguments that *porneia* here should be translated "incest" or "unlawful marriage" in this context, based on Acts 15:29 and 1 Corinthians 5:1, where it clearly means incest.

[2] Linda J. Waite, Don Browning, William J. Doherty, Maggie Gallagher, Luo Ye, and Scott M. Stanley, "Does Divorce Make People Happy?," Institute for American Values, https://www.healthymarriageinfo.org/wp-content/uploads/2018/05/UnhappyMarriages.pdf.

[3] Julie Baumgardner, "Does Divorce Lead to Happiness?," First Things First, May 22, 2018, https://firstthings.org/does-divorce-lead-to-happiness/.

exception of reducing the incidence of marital violence for unhappy spouses (in violent marriages), divorce failed, on average, to result in improvements in psychological well-being for unhappy spouses."[4]

WHY DIDN'T THEY DIVORCE?

When asked why they didn't divorce, a number cited the high cost of divorcing as the reason. Others said they couldn't do that to their children, knowing the devastating effects divorce has been shown to have on children. (More on that later.) A number of men—but no women—cited an intact marriage as key to their vocation as a parent and their ability to protect and love their children.[5]

A good number of people who stayed married even when they were unhappy did so because they had a very negative view of divorce. When they considered divorce, they saw it as far worse than their unhappy marriage. (It is.)

Among those who stayed married despite difficulties, many cited camaraderie as a key element in their happiness. Others mentioned reaching a comfort zone with each other. Several didn't want to be alone. Formerly misbehaving husbands who reformed were "deeply grateful to their wives" for putting up with them for so long.

HOW DID DIFFICULT MARRIAGES IMPROVE?

Gallagher, Waite, and co. saw three main ways things improved: "the marital endurance ethic; the marital work ethic and the personal happiness epic." In the first of these, the couples didn't so much work on

---

[4] Waite, et al., "Does Divorce Make People Happy?," 13.
[5] Ibid., 20.

their problems as survived them. They found that as time wore on, the problems seemed less important and things improved, bringing more happiness. Some wives whose husbands were never home indicated they decided not to complain so much and hang in there. Others just adapted, and found life bearable.[6]

Those with the "marital work ethic" worked on their problems by behaving differently or communicating better. When the problems were solved, life got better. How did they work on problems? By going on more dates together or just finding more time for each other, or by getting help from others, either family members or clergy or marriage counselors. Men often changed to heroically serve their wives and children. This coincides well with the nature of manhood: to strive for virtue and to succeed.[7]

In the "personal happiness" group, the spouses didn't solve their problems; they discovered other ways to find happiness outside their marriage. One wife who told this author she was bored took my suggestion that she find an enjoyable activity to do weekly. She did, and found that life wasn't so bad after all. Many spouses found other interests and friends and their outlook improved.

A number of badly behaving husbands received good advice from family, friends, or clergy. In other cases the wives had others speak to their husbands. One woman told her sister she wanted to divorce, and the sister told her, "You don't want to get a divorce. I've been divorced, I don't think this is what you want. If you want to keep it up, go ahead, but if you don't [want a divorce] knock it off right now." Many pointed to religion as a key factor

---

[6] Ibid., 24–25.
[7] Ibid., 25.

to deter them from divorce. Going to church as a family, and being with other families, helped a great deal.[8]

This, incidentally, is why couples' groups such as Teams of Our Lady can be so effective in keeping couples together. More on this later.

WAKE UP CALLS

One of the biggest devices wives utilized was the "divorce threat." "Many wives (but no husbands)" pointed to their threatening divorce as a key to getting their spouses to behave better. Some husbands agreed that this helped them to reform. Wives utilized outside help far more than did husbands, from divorce lawyers, counselors, or in-laws. And "many wives but no husbands saw themselves as vulnerable to exploitation by their spouses, unless they stood up for themselves and got help from others."[9]

While the mention of divorce and contacting a lawyer often got the attention of an extremely obstinate husband, the authors of the study cautioned against using divorce as "a constant threat," since this can undermine the confidence needed for a good marriage. When mentioning divorce brought about change, the wife's aim was not divorce, but improved behavior, and that was clearly stated.[10]

One husband and wife came to me for counseling when he was ready for change. Alas, she had already decided to divorce him. It was such bad timing, because she had finally gotten his attention and he was ready to reform when she quit. Women have a moral obligation to take some strong measures to get their husbands'

---

[8] Ibid., 26.
[9] Ibid., 27.
[10] Ibid.

attention *before* they are so emotionally drained that they just don't care anymore. *So many marriages could be saved by the wife doing this.*

How does she do it? By saying in as dramatic fashion as possible, "I am very, very unhappy. We need to get counseling right away if we're going to save this marriage; and even then, I can't promise anything." If that doesn't wake him up, she must be ready to (a) get counseling herself and (b) separate as a last resort, with the intent to stir him to save the marriage.

From what I have seen, when a dependable husband says, "I will do anything I can to save this marriage," he usually does.

COUNSELING

Just slightly more than a third of spouses whose marriages had improved reported they had gone for marriage counseling. Most claimed it was the main factor in saving their marriages. Religious counselors rated higher than secular. Alas, some secular marriage counselors encouraged divorce. One reason why priests and ministers were preferred to professional counselors is that they were seen as taking an interest in the couple and their marriage, rather than just charging by the hour.[11]

In the cases where men were behaving badly, value-neutral counseling didn't help. What often helped was when the wife rallied family members, clergy, or divorce attorneys to urge the husband to change.[12]

One thing couples can do themselves, without counseling, is to sit down every month or so and suggest one thing they want each other to do differently. This can work wonders.

---

[11] Ibid., 28–29.
[12] Ibid., 30.

COMMITMENT

One thing that the researchers found was that commitment to a lifelong marriage was a major factor for happiness. This was fully in keeping with findings from other studies, some of which the authors cited. They noted that "commitment, it turns out, is not just a side effect; it is also a cause of relationship happiness." Those who were more willing to consider divorce undermined satisfaction in their marriage and the security of the spouses.[13]

The authors cited "a growing literature on sacrifice"[14] as a great help for marital success. A husband is far more likely to sacrifice for his wife if he is committed to a lifelong marriage.

I have seen many couples who were deeply committed to marriage rebound remarkably from situations that appeared hopeless. One wife was reluctant to do something that would please her husband because he was acting like a jerk. When I asked her to do it to save their marriage, she agreed.

MORE STUDIES

According to an article by The Marriage Place in 2019, a good number of studies indicated that divorce does not make a person happy. "Financial loss, increased risk for depression, suicide, and addiction—not only for you but for your children as well—are all byproducts of divorce. And most of us know the likelihood of divorce increases with each subsequent marriage." The authors agreed that happiness after divorce is possible, but it does not result from the divorce.[15]

---

[13] Ibid., 30–31.
[14] Ibid.
[15] The Marriage Place, "Will Divorce Make Me Happier?," January

It is true that some do become happier after a divorce. However, a good number of marriages that involved such major troubles as alcoholism, infidelity, and emotional decline became happy by working to overcome these issues. Research has shown that a majority of divorced adults are less happy and suffer more psychological stress when compared with married people.[16]

In August 2019, Diana Bruk wrote of a study carried out in the UK which found that women are happier than men after divorce. Thirty-five percent of women claimed a reduction of stress after leaving their spouse and 30 percent reported an increase in self-esteem. Just 17 percent of men saw less stress and 15 percent grew in self-esteem. The underlying reason for this is that 80 percent of divorces are initiated by women.[17]

It should be of interest to many that all those numbers were in the minority. May we assume that 65 percent of women didn't have lower stress and 70 percent saw no increase in self-esteem?

Bruk points out that a good number of men are blindsided by divorce. They thought things were better because the wife stopped complaining. She even gives a link for spouses, "127 Questions to Ask Your Partner About Love, Life, & Intimacy," to avoid getting blindsided.[18]

19, 2019, https://themarriageplace.com/2019/01/will-divorce-make-me-happier/.

[16] Your Divorce Questions, "Will Divorce Make Me Happier?," https://yourdivorcequestions.org/will-divorce-make-me-happier/.

[17] Diana Bruk, "Research Finds Women Are Twice as Likely as Men to Feel Happier Post-Divorce," August 1, 2019, https://bestlifeonline.com/women-happier-after-divorce-survey/.

[18] Diana Bruk and Carrie Weisman, "127 Questions to Ask Your Partner About Love, Life, & Intimacy," *Best Life*, July 13, 2023, https://bestlifeonline.com/questions-to-ask-your-spouse/. The questions are excellent!

* * *

In summary, then, while the grass often looks greener when marriage gets tough, it isn't. In the main study considered, which was authored by highly respected researchers, close to two-thirds of those who stayed in problematic marriages found marital happiness five years later.

So, why not get a divorce? Because God "hates" divorce, and in most cases, it won't make you happy! The answer to a difficult marriage is to seek real help, work at changing yourself, and learn to cope!

CHAPTER III

Communication 101

SARAH GETS OFF THE PHONE WITH her sister and sighs, "Sometimes she drives me nuts."

Her husband Bill says, "You should stop calling that woman."

"She's my sister," Sarah answers, "and she is struggling to raise those five children."

Bill: "She'd have help by now if she had let me fix her up with Jerry."

Sarah: "She's still grieving over Tom's death. She just wasn't ready."

Bill: "It's been two years. She has to move on."

Sarah: "She may well in time. But we can't rush her."

Bill: "Well, I don't like to see you frustrated whenever you talk to her."

Sarah: "She needs someone to talk to, and I'm her closest relative."

Bill: "What about your other sisters?"

Sarah: "Bill, I know you mean well, but I don't need you to solve my problems. Just listen. That's enough."

Bill: "Okay, I'll give it a try." (Smart man, not to try to defend himself.)

Here is the new Bill:

Sarah: "Oooh, what a mess!"

Bill: "Is she okay?"

Sarah: "Freddy is driving her crazy."

Bill: "What's he doing?"

Sarah: "Well, for starters, he's into marijuana. He's also having trouble in school."

Bill: "Grades?"

Sarah: "Yes, and behavioral problems."

Bill: "Ouch. That's hard. She's lucky to have a sister like you."

Sarah: "Thanks. And I'm lucky to have a husband who listens to me."

Bill: "Do you need a hug?"

Sarah: "I do." They hug. "I feel so much better. Thanks for being here for me."

This sort of dialogue reflects one of the most common problems in marital communications. She needs to vent her feelings and talk. He thinks he has to fix her problems. He doesn't. He just needs to listen and to hold her. When a woman is stressed she needs to talk. And their husbands need to listen. Simple.

Men are known to be problem-solvers, so it's hard to remove that hat when the wife wants to talk. But the sooner he learns that, the better off he (and she) will be.

Now, when a man is stressed, he *doesn't* want to talk. He wants to sit and gaze into space, and do nothing. Some good wives, when they see their husbands stressed, try to get them to talk. "That's what I need when *I'm* stressed, so I will help him by talking to him." Not good. Men *don't* want to talk when they are stressed. (There are exceptions to this, of course, but by and large these typical behaviors apply to most men and women.)

TALKING AND LISTENING

When a woman tells her husband about an event, she generally gives three times the detail needed to relate what happened. Her husband should not cut her off. If he is smart, he may say something like, "Sweetheart, I have a suggestion: give me the outline of what happened, including the final outcome, and then tell me the details. I will listen the whole time." Then, of course, he needs to listen attentively.

Something beautiful happens when a man listens carefully to his wife, even though it really tries his patience. He receives intimacy. He gets to know her better. Many wives, and some husbands, too, say they don't know each other anymore. You can't stay in touch with someone, stay intimate with a person, without talking to them and listening to them.

Marriage counselor Scott Haltzman urges men to study their wives the way they might study a project at work. Observe her carefully and see what she likes and dislikes. He invites men to write down what they have learned, and to write their own job description to fulfill their vocation as husband.[1]

Perhaps that's why Mark Gungor says, in one of his *"Laughing Your Way to A Better Marriage"* talks, that a husband should spend some quality time at least each week communicating with his wife. And, he says, "That usually means, she talks and you listen."[2]

Happiness in marriage, it seems, is directly proportional to intimacy. If you are close to your spouse, if you often spend time talking and listening, you are likely to have a happy marriage. If you see marriage

---

[1] Scott Haltzman, *The Secrets of Happily Married Men* (San Francisco: Jossey-Bass, 2006), 64.

[2] "Mark Gungor Full Marriage Seminar," YouTube video, posted by "Bro James," January 13, 2017, https://www.youtube.com/watch?v=n-WkPOFz3RSk. A hilarious and insightful presentation on marriage. There are some flaws in his presentation: he suggests a husband should be nice to his wife in order to have more sex (rather than because he vowed to love her), and he is confused about unconditional love. Otherwise, his message is great.

as some sideline, which often interferes with your golf game or your night out with the boys, you will likely be unhappy. The investment you make in your spouse, both in time and communication, will be richly rewarded.

MALE THICKNESS

If women can try men's patience by giving too much detail, men can try women's patience by being slow to respond to their wife's requests. When a woman asks a man to clean out the garage or remove the mouse from the mousetrap and he fails to do so, she must realize that it is usually not bad will that holds him back. It's male thickness. We just don't seem to get it on the first request, and in some cases, on the first five requests.

Women must ordinarily ask a man several times for it to register. The key for the Christian woman is to ask just as sweetly the seventh or eighth time as the first. When women start to get mean and nasty about their requests, they are less—not more—likely to get him to do what they want. Remember, it's not bad will on the man's part, just thickness. Would it help to have a "honey-do" list on a board in the kitchen? Yes, absolutely. It might help him to remember.

Women will say, "I shouldn't have to keep asking him." True, you shouldn't, but for most men, you must. That's normal.

Should men try to respond to their wife's requests the first or second time as a penance, and to grow in holiness? Yes, of course! That could save some souls and bring a husband a great deal of grace.

And along the same lines, a woman should never think she can get a man to respond to a subtle hint.

Impossible. She needs to spell out exactly what she wants. Hints are generally lost on men.

COMMUNICATION FOR GOOD MARITAL RELATIONS

Wives often complain that their husbands ask to have marital relations shortly after they have had a disagreement, and they haven't made up yet. As a result, they say "I feel like a prostitute" if they comply. So what's a woman to do?

Let's use an example to explore possible solutions to the problem. Melvin and Sarah had a rather ugly disagreement after dinner and now they are in bed.

First, she has to put on her humility hat. She feels like he's really at fault, and perhaps he is, but if she points that out to him, he'll get defensive again and things will continue to be miserable. So she has to offer the olive branch. (It's always the Christian, or the one who is more Christian, who initiates healing, regardless of who is more at fault.) She has to be highly motivated to want to repair the relationship. She's doing this for God, for her children. She's doing this because she promised to love this man in good times *and in bad* and things have really been bad lately.

So, there they are in bed. Melvin says or does something to indicate he'd like to have sexual relations.

Sarah responds to his initiative, "I'd like to have relations but could we talk first?" (She offers him some hope and upholds his fragile ego.)

He may say "Do we have to?"

(This is a belligerent answer, and there may be more, but she has to glide right over these if she wants to get to the goal. She's got to be positive no matter what he says.) "Well, you know how it is: men like to have sex;

women like to talk. [Pause.] You wouldn't want me to have relations with you in a mechanical way. Don't you like it better when I'm really into it? [Pause.] It wouldn't take long..." she says sweetly as she puts her hand on his shoulder. This is another way of softening him up.

"Talk about what?"

"About you." (Again, she ignores his boorishness.) She really wants to say, "About us," but he would be too defensive to accept that right now. "I don't think you're happy." She's really unhappy herself, but if she makes him happy, he may make her happy. Here comes the clincher, one that will bring her buckets of grace. "It's very important to me to make you happy, and I'm not sure just how to do it. Our emotions have been kind of raw lately. Everything we do seems to cause us pain. I really want for us to stop hurting each other, but I need you to help me know what I can do. Please, tell me one thing I can do differently to give you some relief." (Notice she asks for just *one thing* to do. Never leave it open-ended so that he can read off a laundry list.)

"Okay, when I come home every evening, how about a warm welcome? I have trouble dealing with all your problems in addition to the ones I've been facing all day, the minute I walk in. It stresses me out." His answer may be less diplomatic than this, but she still has to be ready for whatever he says. No criticism.

"You're right. I have to work on that. I'm sorry I've been so thoughtless." (No excuses at this point—things are going well. Don't ruin it.) "I promise I'll make that a priority from now on." She starts to caress his arm. She remains silent for a few seconds.

He may say, "Is that it?"

"Almost. Do I get one?" she asks softly.

"Sure," he says. He's warming up now and he kind of likes the caressing.

"Every night, after we put the kids down, hold me and ask me how I am. If I've had a hard day, tell me you're sorry I had such a hard day and that you're there for me. Hold me tight for a minute or two and tell me you love me."

"I can do that. I'll do it!" he says. Men love to be needed. "Why didn't we have this conversation before?" he asks himself.

He's warmed up completely by now—she could have asked for more. But not to worry. She'll have other chances.

"Hey," she says, still caressing his arm, "let's celebrate our marriage covenant."

"That sounds like a theological way of saying we should do what I had in mind in the first place."

"You're another Thomas Aquinas."

Et cetera, et cetera, et cetera. They didn't solve every problem, but they solved a major one: they made peace. They communicated without getting angry.

Notice too, they didn't ask for the moon, but each asked for something personal, something so simple (and so typically important!). She's going to get some support; he's going to be able to relax when he gets home.

And, of course, the next time the issue of marital relations comes up, if he's smart he'll begin by asking, "How are you? How did things go today?" One husband began to ask his wife this the moment they arrived in bed at night. She absolutely loved it and since he did it every night it took her just ten minutes to express everything. Their marital covenant celebrations were sizzling (i.e., amazing sex).

DATES

One thing that every book on marriage recommends is that the couple should regularly go on dates. "Why do we have to go on dates? We live together!" You may live together, but that doesn't mean you talk to each other. When you go on a date, you have to talk, and talking is key to your intimacy.

Claudia and David Arp, authors of *Ten Great Dates to Energize Your Marriage*, write,

> When was the last time you talked to your spouse for thirty uninterrupted minutes? Would you like to have more fun with your spouse? Is dating something you only did before you were married?
>
> We believe that having a healthy, growing marriage relationship requires friendship, fun and romance. And, there's no better way to encourage all these things than having dates! . . . Great dates involve communicating with one another, reviving the spark that initially ignited your fire, and developing mutual interests and goals that are not focused on your careers or your children. Great dates can revitalize your relationship.[3]

The Arps note that an experiment was done to determine how much time the average couple spends communicating each week. The results? Just seventeen minutes a week. That's a recipe for divorce!

Here are some of their recommendations for dates:

1. Agree on having ten dates.
2. Schedule the dates, and tell each other via words or little notes that you are looking forward to the next date.

---

[3] Dave Arp and Claudia Arp, *Ten Great Dates to Energize Your Marriage* (Grand Rapids: Zondervan, 1997), 12.

3. Don't discuss problems or the children on the date.
4. Stay positive. Hold hands. You can do this walking and talking or cuddling on a bench somewhere.[4]

They also conducted their own national survey on marriage and discovered three common elements in healthy marriages: (1) the marriage relationship is held as more important than any other relationship, (2) both partners are committed to "growing and changing together," and (3) "they work at staying close."[5]

Gary Smalley learned principle number one the hard way. He came home for lunch one day and his wife was unresponsive. He asked her if something was wrong and she said it wouldn't do any good to discuss it. He didn't get it. He persevered and in time she told him he placed little importance on her. "You'd rather be at work, or with your friends, or counseling people than spending time with me." She told him, "If someone calls you when we have plans, you're liable to say, 'Let me check with my wife and see if I can't postpone our plans.' I just can't believe you would do that to me over and over again."[6]

At this point he told her it was easier to move his plans with her than to move other people. (Big mistake.) She went on to give him more examples. Finally, he got it. He asked forgiveness, and promised to change. She was skeptical. She had "heard that song before."

What he writes next is telling:

---

[4] Ibid., 14–15.
[5] Ibid., 23–24.
[6] Gary Smalley, *If Only He Knew; What No Woman Can Resist* (Grand Rapids, MI: Zondervan, 1998), 39.

I wanted to tell her she was the most important person in my life. I really *wanted* to feel
that way. At first I didn't have those feelings
but I *wanted* to have them. As I tried to make
her more important to me than anyone else, I
soon began to *feel* she was top priority...

The most important way I have ever
expressed my love to Norma was when I
finally attached a high value to her, when I
decided that next to my relationship with
God . . . she is worth more to me than anything on this earth—and she knows it.[7]

Later on, Smalley took a lesser job at his company
because his work was interfering with his family life.
It paid off. He got much closer to his wife and family,
and after a few months he was given a new job in the
same company, better than the one he had given up.[8]

CUT THE CRITICISM

Gary Smalley reaped the fruit of his criticizing
one day when he and the family were watching a
football game and his wife Norma made sandwiches
for everyone but him. Later on, when he asked her
why, she had a great answer: "Do you realize that
every time I make you a sandwich you say something
critical about it? 'Norma, you didn't give me enough
lettuce.... Is this avocado ripe? You put too much
mayonnaise on this....' I just wasn't up to being crit-
icized the other day..."[9]

He thought to himself, it wasn't really *every* time.
He kept his mouth shut, however, having learned that
when a spouse says "every time," she does not intend

---

[7] Ibid., 41.
[8] Ibid., 50–51.
[9] Ibid., 110–11.

mathematical precision. She just means "a lot." Well, he stopped criticizing, and started praising, and now he gets lots of good sandwiches.[10]

I told one wife there should be two praises for every criticism in her marriage. She put this into practice, and things improved dramatically. This should be the rule not only in every marriage, but every relationship. Being hypercritical is a trap every Christian—indeed, every person—should work hard to avoid.

One youth basketball player lamented that his coach was always telling him—and his teammates—what he had done wrong, and what he should have done. They would have been far more motivated, he said, if the coach had also praised them when they did things right.

John Gottman says that criticism is an attack on the person, not just the behavior. And it usually includes blame. Complaining, on the other hand, is saying something negative about how you would like things to be. Gottman gives an example: For a spouse to say, "We don't go out as much as I'd like to," is a complaint. "You never take me anywhere" is a criticism. Actually, "It would be so nice to go out together more," sounds even better.[11]

Gottman suggests that a person voice dissatisfaction by making "I" statements rather than "you" statements. It really makes quite a difference in communicating discontent. Just about every book on marriage encourages spouses to use these "I" statements for a complaint. Which sounds better, "You forgot to take out the garbage and now the kitchen stinks," or "I was hoping you'd take the garbage out last night"?

---

[10] Ibid., 111.
[11] Gottman, *Why Marriages Succeed or Fail*, 75–76. Gottman's book is referred to in many books on marriage.

More examples: "I was hurt by that statement," or, "I love it when you put the kids to bed," or, "I would really like you to come home earlier on Wednesdays." Always begin with the pronoun "I" when you have a complaint, and you'll avoid a ton of marital misery.[12]

Laura Doyle, in her book *The Surrendered Wife*, has an even better idea. She suggests wives just say "I want a new car" or "I would like to go out more."[13] I think she could put the first request a bit more gently, such as "You know, I would really love to have a new car," but the concept is sound. Better to ask for what you want than to complain that you lack something.

Of course, the hardest part of communication is often expressing dissatisfaction. Saying "You pig, you left your dirty socks out again," will never win an award for diplomacy. But saying "You are probably in the top 10 percent of husbands in this country. If you could remember to put your socks in the hamper, you'd be in the top 5 percent," just might.

Arnold Palmer was a great golfer. But he was also known as a crowd pleaser, because he was always kind to the crowds that followed him. One classic example is when he was trying to putt and the spectators were being noisy. It clearly irritated him, and as I watched on television, I wondered how he would handle this diplomatically. He stood up, walked over toward the stands, smiled and put his fingers on his lips, saying "Shhhhh." He kept his cool and he kept his fans.

Some claim, "Well, Father, diplomacy is not my strong point." It's no one's strong point until they start cultivating it. It's like saying in fifth grade,

---

[12] Ibid., 74.
[13] Laurra Doyle, *The Surrendered Wife* (New York: Simon & Schuster, 2001), 80–81.

"Calculus is not my strong point." It's something you learn, not an infused virtue or an inherited personality trait. More on diplomacy in a moment.

FOUR MARRIAGE KILLERS

John Gottman identifies four things that destroy a marriage. He calls them the "Four Horsemen of the Apocalypse." The first is criticism, which we already discussed.

Contempt

The second horseman is contempt. This goes beyond criticism to "insult and psychologically abuse your partner." He gives the example of a couple arguing about spending. After many heated exchanges about the subject, she finally yells, "Why are you so irresponsible? You never pay attention to how much you spend. You are so selfish!"

He answers, "Oh shut up! You're just a stingy cheapskate who doesn't know how to live. I don't know how I ended up with you anyway."[14]

I am amazed to hear how many *Christian* spouses get into such abusive speech. I am equally amazed at how many of these same couples are able to forgive and learn to stop such shameful behavior. How true is the adage "familiarity breeds contempt"! Of course, it need not. Contempt is a serious violation of the vow each spouse made to "love and honor you . . ."

John van Epp, in his book *How to Avoid Marrying a Jerk*, suggests observing the way your boyfriend/girlfriend treats his/her parents, his/her family members, waiters, taxi drivers, dog, and previous sweethearts. Why? Because after a good number of years people

---

[14] Gottman, *Why Marriages Succeed or Fail*, 79.

often treat their spouses the way they treat these other people they have lived with for a lengthy period of time. I would call it the familiarity syndrome. So, if you had bad relationships with family members, you need to work hard at avoiding some of the same patterns with your spouse after some years of marriage. Think long and hard about avoiding any contemptuous behavior toward your spouse that you may have had with family members and others you were close to.

There is another reason for this familiarity syndrome: failure to make a habit out of often thanking your partner and praising him/her. These two things are essential parts of love. From what I have seen, couples who struggle with contempt tend to coast after some years instead of continuing to build their relationship. Loving someone involves trying to make the beloved's life better, and being thankful and praising this person are beautiful ways of doing that.

Consider the Psalms, our songs of love for God: they are constantly thanking and praising God. Granted, God is more worthy of our thanks and praise, but married couples take a vow to "love and honor" each other all the days of their lives. Two key elements of loving your spouse are to praise and thank him/her. You can make these a habit.

"*What if I don't feel like doing these things?*" So your love is conditional? Did you mention the need to *feel like* loving this person when you made your wedding vows? Vows you made before God? How many, many marriages have been saved by *one* person setting about to fulfill their own vows, regardless of what the spouse was doing.

"*What will my reward be for doing this?*" Your reward may or may not come from your spouse. But your guaranteed reward will be from God. Anytime we do God's will, especially when it is difficult, we will be rewarded by him. It may not be right away, or in the way we expect, but it will come. "[God] will give to each according to his works" (Rom 2:6). Loving your (difficult) spouse—and everyone else—for God's sake is the only sure way to success and happiness.

Defensiveness

Gottman suggests that defensiveness is the third "horseman." This is a common tactic of husbands when they are attacked, but wives can use it, too. He says this takes several forms: denying responsibility; making excuses; blaming the other; tit-for-tat ("You did this." "Yes, but you did that."); whining ("You never . . ."); etc. Defensiveness never solves an argument; it just escalates it.[15]

There are two solutions to defensiveness. She needs to remember that most men mess up out of clumsiness, not bad will. And he needs to remember that she's not out to get him. If she says, "You forgot to take out the garbage last night," or "You haven't removed that dead snake from the garden," he could answer simply, "I'm sorry. I need to get at that." (Of course, she would have done better to say, "Honey, my prince, please remember to take out the garbage," or "I am hoping my big, brave husband will take away the dead snake in the garden.")

I was playing basketball one evening and the guy I was guarding said, "The next time you guard me so closely I'm going to punch you in the mouth." I simply answered "Sorry." He was so surprised, he had me repeat it to make sure he had heard me correctly!

---

[15] Ibid., 84–89.

Stonewalling

Stonewalling is the fourth horseman. This is when one spouse, usually the husband, just shuts up. He doesn't want to argue any more so he just does not answer. He is quiet. She feels like she is talking to a stone wall. Gottman claims that men do this more than women because men's blood pressure and pulse rate rise more during an argument.[16]

Perhaps an alternative to stonewalling would be for the husband to say to his nagging wife, "You know, I could really use a hug right now." As he holds her gently in his arms he might say, "Honey, let's sit and talk about that . . . *holding hands.*"

The point of all this is that couples should be very aware of each of these bad tactics and be committed to avoiding them. Avoid them like the plague! The relationship is almost always of higher priority than the subject of these arguments.

SOME EXAMPLES

Here are some examples of good—and bad—communication. One woman told her husband, "You did that wrong," and got an icy response. Had she said, "You probably should have done that differently," she might have avoided the ice.

"You are too tough on Jimmy" could be replaced by "I think you might get better results from Jimmy if you were a bit gentler with him." Or, "I hate it when you use that word" might better be said as "I would love you to eliminate that word from your vocabulary." Or, "You never ask how I am doing," versus "You know, I would really like you to just ask me how I am doing from time to time." "You never tell me how you are

---

[16] Ibid., 93–95.

feeling," versus "I would love it if you shared your feelings with me more often." These are some suggestions for wives.[17]

For husbands: "You care only about the children; not me" could be "I would love to spend more time together, just the two of us." "You never thank me for anything," versus "You know, when you thank me for some of the things I do, I am inspired to do more for you." "You nag me whenever I have a free moment" could be "Let's make a list of things I need to get done and prioritize it (perhaps on a whiteboard)."[18]

POSITIVE INTERACTIONS

John Gottman studied married couples and concluded that for a marriage to be successful, there need to be five times as many positive interactions as negative interactions. For example, if a couple had a big argument, there should be five positive interactions to balance that, such as a sweet apology, holding hands, playing footsie while at the breakfast table or in bed, hugs, words of praise.[19]

Would it be better to just avoid these hot issues? No. You need to air differences. When Gottman studied marriages in which there were hardly any conflicts, after three years of marriage, they were not as happy as those who aired their differences, even with anger. However, that ratio of five-to-one

---

[17] Adam Bunger, "7 Common Complaints Wives Have About Their Husbands, According to Therapists," *Fatherly*, October 7, 2022, https://www.fatherly.com/life/common-complaints-wives-have-about-husbands.

[18] Debra McLeod, "The 8 Most Common Complaints Unhappy Husbands Have About Their Wives According to a Relationship Coach and Mediator," *Your Tango*, October 17, 2022, https://www.yourtango.com/heartbreak/common-complaints-unhappy-husbands-wives.

[19] Gottman, *Why Marriages Succeed or Fail*, 56–58.

positive-to-negative had to be maintained for the marriage to work.[20]

Gottman says the basic ingredients for a good marriage are love and respect. Let's make sure we understand both those words. "Love" doesn't mean "like." It means you are concerned for the good of your spouse, and you see your role as someone called to make his/her life truly better. And respect comes right out of the marriage vows: "I will love and *honor* you all the days of my life."

This brings us to another important issue: being polite. I asked one wife to observe the manners she and her husband showed toward each other each day. She was shocked to find they were really quite rude, hardly ever saying please or thank you. They started working on being polite and things got better and better.

A young couple came to me to prepare them for marriage. When I brought up the issue of politeness, the fiancée smiled and said that John didn't believe in it. He thought it was too formal. I suggested that after they were married for a year or two without being polite, he might think quite differently. I have never heard a couple in our monthly couples groups downplay the value of courtesy. These men and women are veterans of marriage, and they know well the importance of good manners.

Always say please, or "if you would be so kind," when asking for something. (The latter is helpful if you forget to start a request with "please.") And be lavish in thanking your partner for what they do. One wife asked, "Why should I thank him for just doing what he is supposed to do?" I answered, "Because you

---

[20] Ibid., 66.

should be grateful for him doing what he's supposed to do. And, if you thank him, he will probably keep doing it—and more." Some husbands do not do what they are supposed to do!

Another thing about communication. Don't sweat the small stuff. I am always amazed at the petty things people argue about. I asked one wife what she and her husband had such a big argument about and she said, "I don't remember. It wasn't anything important." It hardly ever is.

One young man, after reading a book on marriage, said, "I could never remember all these things. It won't work." First of all, you work on only one or two things at a time to start. Secondly, when you make some of these things a habit, you don't have to remember. They become automatic.

But, make no mistake about it, it's not easy to change your behavior. The people in these stories who changed and improved their marriage had to work hard at it. What they did sounds easy, but it's not. Changing takes a lot of effort, and requires lots of the three most important virtues for a moral life (according to St. Augustine): (1) humility, (2) humility, and (3) humility. Marriage is a great institution in which to learn this particular virtue, which happens to be a prerequisite to enter God's Kingdom.

* * *

In summary then, husbands, when your wife expresses her frustration, there is no need to solve her problems; just listen and express compassion and sympathy. Wives, when your husband is stressed, know that this is a time when he *does not* want to talk. Men just want to go blank for twenty to thirty minutes or more—even hours—and think about nothing. Let 'em be.

Husbands, when your wife wants to tell you what happened, and she tells you three times as much as she needs to for you to get the picture, know that she is not unique. Most women do that. Rather than cut her off and ruin her story, better to ask for the conclusion and then for the details. Then, listen attentively to what she says, as a way to build intimacy. Remember, the more you communicate with your wife, the more intimacy you will have and the more she will love you. The more intimacy you have, the happier you will be.

Husbands, study your wife and learn what things make her happy. Try to have a good conversation with her at least once a week and let her do most of the talking. You won't regret it.

Wives, your turn to practice patience is when you ask your husband six times to do something and he doesn't do it. The expression, "I shouldn't have to keep asking him" may be true, but it betrays a great naïveté with regard to men. That is the way most men operate, or in this case, do not operate. The key for wives is to ask the tenth time just as sweetly as you asked the first time. And the key for men is to do what their wife asks them the first or second time as part of their journey to holiness.

Husbands and wives, expect your sexual intimacy to blossom beautifully as you communicate more and more. Wives, give your husbands half an hour to unwind and do nothing when they arrive home. Husbands, be sure to hold your wives while they tell you how they are feeling. (And, of course, just listen. Don't try to fix her.)

Go on lots of dates, romantic dates. Men, you should ask your wife out on a date, and it should be something you have planned. Make her number one. And for both of you, stop criticizing. Two praises for every criticism. If you have a legitimate complaint, begin with the word "I" (such as "I feel so hurt when you belittle me"). And think hard about how to express dissatisfaction diplomatically.

If you want your marriage to work, you must have five positive interactions (like hugs or tender kisses) for every negative interaction (like a big argument). Five! Honor your spouse by being polite: always say please and thank you. And don't sweat the small stuff in your marriage.

Finally, don't think it will be easy to change and do all these things. It takes lots of effort and humility. The kind of effort and humility you need to be saved.

CHAPTER IV

What Is Love?
(The 4 Meanings of Love)[1]

ONE DAY I WAS DISCUSSING WITH a parishioner her relationship with her husband. She said she really didn't love him much anymore. I asked her if she was concerned for his good, and she replied she was. "Then, you love him. *That* is the love you pledged on your wedding day, not some romantic feeling. When you tell him you love him, that should be the primary meaning of the love you profess."

"I haven't told him I love him in a long time," she admitted.

"Well, don't you think you should? After all, you promised to love him for as long as you both shall live."

"I don't know if I can bring myself to say it now," she replied.

Clearly, he had hurt her over the years, and she believed she had to *feel* it before she could say it. Ironically, couples often come to feel it again only when they say it first and work at it again. In any event, she was clearly confused over the meaning of love. I have encountered many other instances of this confusion over the years, some of which have been nearly catastrophic.

---

[1] This chapter is an adaptation of chapter two of the author's book, *Christian Courtship in an Oversexed World*, originally published by *Our Sunday Visitor*, and now published in its revised edition titled *Christian Dating in A Godless World* (Sophia Press, 2016).

In order to understand marital love, it's important for us to try to eliminate the confusion in the English language regarding the different meanings of love. There are, alas, several meanings of the word love, for which the Greeks had four different words. The first, *agape* ("ah-GAH-pay"), is often translated as "divine love" because it is typified by the self-sacrificial love of God for mankind. The second, *philia*, is friendship, or "brotherly love." The third, *storge* ("STOR-gay"), is affection, often called "familial" love. The fourth, *eros*, is emotional love. C. S. Lewis wrote a classic explanation of these four dynamics of love, entitled (oddly enough) *The Four Loves*. I will use some of his ideas as a starting point.

AGAPE

The love that a man and woman pledge for each other on their wedding day is divine love, or as the Greeks called it, *agape*. This is the most important of the four since it is the condition for salvation: "You shall love the Lord your God with all your heart, with all your soul, with all your strength, and with all your mind" (Lk 10:27). The Greek word used here in Luke is *agapao*, a derivative of *agape*. Since it is something commanded, it must be a voluntary act, not a feeling. We might define it as: *a giving of self for the good of the beloved without conditions.* Another way to put it would be: *an active concern for the good of the beloved which is unconditional.*

If you love in this way, you give of your time, your money, your effort, whatever you have, for the one you love. But you don't give indiscriminately. You give only insofar as it is for the *good* of the one you love. Giving so as to please the other may be divine love, but not necessarily, since what pleases a person is not always what is good for him (or her, understood).

The father who says no to his son when he asks for a Mercedes on his sixteenth birthday is showing him love. The woman who says no to her boyfriend when he asks for immoral activity is showing him love. God himself gives us tough love when we turn from his way and our life falls apart.

There are no "ifs" in this sort of love. "If you behave," or "if you continue to please me," or "if you don't get fat," have no place here. A mother loves her child in this consistent way, always ready to work for his good, whether the child pleases her or not.

God himself doesn't like us much when we sin, but he will always take us back, because he is a God of merciful love. His active concern for our good involves no conditions, and he expects us to love in the same way.

Agape is usually expressed in quiet, enduring ways, without much fanfare: fifty years of doing her family's laundry, forty years of ministering to the sick and dying, decades of little sacrifices for wife and children, a lifelong commitment to prayer and teaching young children. As such, this is the least exciting, and even the most potentially boring of the loves. But it is the most powerful and most rewarding in the long run.

It's like watering a small tree. You care for it day after day, week after week, year after year, and the growth is hardly noticeable. You have only a vague hope for a reward. Then one day, after many years, the tree blossoms, and finally it bears fruit. It is only then, after all that seemingly endless effort, that you come to realize it was all worth it. In fact, agape is the only type of love that can fulfill us as persons. Pope John Paul II writes:

> Man cannot live without love. He remains a
> being that is incomprehensible for himself,
> his life is senseless, if love is not revealed to
> him, if he does not encounter love, if he does
> not experience it and make it his own, if he
> does not participate intimately in it.[2]

We see this love in the wife or husband who has
been deeply disappointed by his/her spouse, and yet
puts that aside to try to make peace and heal the
relationship. We see it in friends or relatives who
have been married twenty-five years or more. They've
been through the years together, the hurts so typical
of any human relationship, and the hardships of life.
And now, because their love was truly unconditional,
and they continued to love when it ceased being fun
for a time, they have something special. There's a
certain peace, a glow in their marriage. This is the
way of agape.

Although agape is an outward movement, a giving
of self, those who love in this way ordinarily receive
it as well.[3] So, even though agape most often involves
receiving as well as giving, the Christian will always
emphasize giving more than receiving.

The most profound expression of this divine love
is to give "when it hurts." Christ put it very directly:
"A man can have no greater love than to lay down his
life for his friends" (Jn 15:13). He preached this love,
lived by it, and died by it. By his grace, we too can
live and die by it.

---

[2] *Redemptor Hominis.*
[3] If loving a person in this way does not bring about a response
because of a lack on the part of the beloved, God promises us a
reward nonetheless.

CONJUGAL OR CHOICE LOVE

The verb form of *agapao* is occasionally used in the New Testament to speak of a choice. Christ said, "No man can serve two masters. He will either hate one and love the other or be attentive to one and despise the other" (Mt 6:24). That is, he will *choose* either one or the other. Thus, there is a love that might be called "choice love" or "choice agape." It is this love we are to have for God, for he would have us choose him above all other things. Our love for God should be marked by four characteristics: first, *permanence*, in that it should be an everlasting commitment; second, *exclusiveness*, in that we should love no other person to the extent that we love God, i.e., with all our heart, soul, and mind; third, *being public*, in that we should give witness to this love to others; and fourth, *fruitfulness*, in that it should bear fruit in our sharing God's life of grace in us.

Although this choice love for God is unique, there is another love that reflects it: the conjugal love of marriage. Conjugal love is meant to have the same four marks: *permanence*, in that it should be a lifelong commitment; *exclusiveness*, in that each has but one spouse; *public*, in that couples marry in public and make known their commitment, living it out in public; and *fruitfulness*, in that it is ordered to the begetting of new life.[4] In these ways the conjugal love in marriage symbolizes to the world the (conjugal) love between a person and God.[5]

---

[4] Pope Paul VI speaks of conjugal love having certain traits: human, total, faithful, exclusive until death, and fecund (fruitful) in *Humanae Vitae* 9. I added *public* as another mark which, although less theological, seems to fit our practical discussion here.

[5] As described in Isaiah 62:4–6.

While conjugal love can be expressed in any of the ways agape is expressed, there is one way that is unique to it: bodily communion. With the Lord this involves receiving the Eucharist. With spouses it involves sexual intercourse.

SEXUAL INTIMACY

Sexual intimacy is a sacred, physical sign of the conjugal agape of marriage. As such, it should share the same four marks:

1. Permanence: The sex act itself cries out for a tomorrow, i.e., a marital commitment.

2. Exclusiveness: What decent person would be comfortable sharing his or her sex partner?

3. Public: Although the act does not ordinarily take place in public (thank goodness), husband and wife don't usually hide the fact that they sleep together.

4. Fruitfulness: The act is ordered toward accepting nature's offer of new life. Children are the fruit of married love and give witness to that love for all eternity.

Why is there so much pleasure in sex? The most obvious reason for pleasure in sex is to encourage the propagation of the human race. However, this cannot be the only reason, since the sex act and its pleasure are licit and good during times when procreation is impossible—for example, after menopause, during infertile times, or in the case of sterility.

I would submit, therefore, that the pleasure of sex is also intended as an encouragement to make the commitment of conjugal love and to keep it.

Sexual communion, as Eucharistic communion, is both a crown and a source: a crown for making the marital commitment, and a source of encouragement to keep that commitment.

FRIENDSHIP (*PHILIA*)

Friendship is essentially a relationship based on sharing a common interest.[6] If two people share the same faith, the same politics, the same taste in music, in entertainment, in sports, in intellectual pursuits, they are likely to enjoy spending time together. Lewis rightly points out that while *eros* is face to face, friendship is "side by side."[7] It is best when shared with others, not just between two, because there is an aspect of Doug that is brought out only by John or Susan. And Doug brings out something in Susan that John does not.[8]

Ordinarily, friends contribute more or less equally to the relationship. However, at times one or the other may be wounded, and unable to give. This is when agape, that self-giving love which is the support of all the loves, must take over. A friend is there for his friend in time of need. During such a time he may receive nothing at all from the friendship, except perhaps the knowledge that the relationship was more than a business deal. It was rather an image of our friendship with God.

St. Augustine held friendship to be the highest of the three human loves (agape being divine). Which of the human loves could be more important to a marriage? To share the same faith, the same education, the same values, the same recreational interests, the same taste: these are things on which good marriages are built and without which they may suffer. For him to take dancing lessons because she loves to

---

[6] C. S. Lewis, *The Four Loves* (New York: Harcourt, Brace, Jovanovich, 1960), 96.

[7] Ibid., 91.

[8] Ibid., 92.

dance, for her to study football because he loves the game . . . these are ways to build a friendship for the sake of the committed conjugal love of marriage.

This is not to say married people shouldn't have things they do separately, without their spouse. They should, but there should be many things they do together, to reinforce their friendship.

For a married couple, the friendship should be deep. In other words, each should be able to share their deep inner thoughts and desires, their feelings, their hopes and fears.

To speak of intimate things, each must be interested in the words of the other. When you pour out your heart to someone and they respond, "Where shall we go for dinner tomorrow?" you know there's a problem. Each must respect and want to support the other. If there's fear of rejection, the words of intimacy won't flow. And, when these things are shared, there's careful listening and real openness.[9] Those who meditate a great deal in prayer, those who are comfortable with silence and need not have the radio or television going at all times, those who read—especially spiritual books—are generally much more prepared for intimacy than those who are not into these things.

The sharing of intimacy occurs most easily when the two are together alone and there's lots of time. That's why it's so important that married couples often go on dates. Going out to dinner and sitting off in a secluded part of a quiet restaurant can be a great place for this, or going on a long walk on the beach in the evening. Certainly, when one or the other is in a time of crisis, or suffering a loss, this is a time that lends itself to

[9] Neil Clark Warren, *Finding The Love of Your Life* (Colorado Springs, CO: Focus on The Family, 1998), 109.

intimate conversation.[10] The couples who have shared
their failures and struggles will generally have a far
more intimate relationship than those who have not.

One of the most important things a married couple
shares is raising children. Children are a wonderful common interest of parents, and thus contribute greatly to
their friendship. Children should never be seen as interfering with the love of parents, but a way of fostering it.
This is why couples should not delay having children
to give themselves "time to get to know each other,"
which often really means "time to enjoy each other
without interference." Children will draw the parents
more deeply into that self-giving agape, which is the
source of all happiness, and more deeply into intimate
friendship, the highest of the human loves. A love that
tries to exclude others, i.e., children, without a really
important reason, even for a time, fosters selfishness.

How precious is friendship! "A faithful friend is
a sturdy shelter: he that has found one has found a
treasure... A faithful friend is an elixir of life; and
those who fear the Lord will find [one]" (Sir 6:14).

AFFECTION (*STORGE*)

Affection is sometimes called familial love because
it commonly occurs among family members, but it
is most important in marriage in particular. It is a
tenderness, a gentle caring for someone.

Affection is expressed in many ways: a hug; a tender kiss on the lips, the cheek, or forehead; a tender
smile; a gentle touch on the arm, the hand, the hair.
It seems that good, selfless, chaste affection has been
a casualty in our over-sexed world. Many have lost
the art of affection.

---

[10] Ibid., 112.

Years ago Ann Landers took a survey of her married women readers, asking whether they would prefer to be "cuddled" or to have "the act." Over 70 percent preferred to be cuddled. I don't think this is because they didn't like the act, but because they hadn't been cuddled in a while.

Often, wives tell me that all their husbands want to do is have sex. When I ask them, "Did you have sex together before marriage?" they inevitably answer, "Yes."

Therein lies the problem. They never developed the habit of sharing affection, as an end in itself. When a man has sex with his woman before marriage, he often sees kissing and touching as merely an introduction to sexual intercourse. Wives need to help their husbands realize the great importance of affection in a good marriage. Husbands and wives need to be able to touch, hug, kiss, and be kissed without this being a prelude to sexual activity.

One young man about thirty years old called me after one of our "Christian Dating in An Oversexed World" seminars, and asked, "Well, Father, what should I do to tell my sweetheart goodnight?" Good question.

I told him, "Well, you might put your hand to her face and move forward ever-so-slowly, and gently kiss her once . . . twice . . . three times. Then give her a big, slow hug, pressing your cheek against hers and feeling the warmth as a way of proclaiming your real warm feelings for her. Then, perhaps say something nice, such as, "You are so precious to me." Then say goodnight and kiss her once more, slowly, tenderly, as if you fear she might break if you aren't careful."

"Not bad, Father, not bad," he responded.

"It's been a while, but I have a good memory."

This, of course, was in the context of courtship, not marriage. However, for a husband to kiss his wife like this occasionally could probably do wonders for her heart, which in turn would do wonders for his marital happiness! Women can have their hearts deeply stirred by such a manifestation of romantic affection and the man who performs such will receive mega-feminine rewards.

Of course, there are many other ways to share affection in marriage. My father would always gently kiss my mother before every meal. Several hugs a day are recommended by virtually all marriage counselors.

Studies have shown that lengthy hugging (twenty seconds or more) in marriage has a measurable beneficial effect on the partners, including the production of oxytocin (a bonding chemical), reduced blood pressure, and a reduction in cortisol (a stress hormone) in the woman.[11] They found that the effect in the woman is stronger, but something happens in the man as well. One young husband told me, "I can just feel the tension of the workday melting away at about sixteen seconds into the hug." Couples should aim for at least one twenty-second hug every day.

A husband might reach for his wife's hand and kiss it from time to time. When they walk, they might hold hands or put their arms around each other as they go along.

He might put his hand to her face gently as they lie facing each other in bed at night. He could hold her hands for a minute or two when out to dinner.

When a woman initiates a hug or another form of affection it thrills the heart of the average man. She

---

[11] "How Hugs Can Aid Women's Hearts," *BBC News Channel*, August 8, 2005, http://news.bbc.co.uk/2/hi/4131508.stm.

might put her head on his shoulder while watching a movie. Or, she might touch him tenderly on the hand or kiss him gently on the cheek. Another possibility: taking his hand and putting it around her waist, or just putting her arm in his, and leaning lightly against him as they walk along.

One Catholic husband told his wife, "Tell Fr. Morrow we took his advice and sat on the couch with my head on your lap and shared a lovely evening!" I convinced one wife to buy a bottle of wine and a special loaf of bread for a home date. They lit a candle on the coffee table, put their feet up and sipped wine with their bread as they shared their thoughts. The husband urged her to come to see me more often for marriage advice!

One of the best articles I have ever read on couples sharing affection was written by Peter McFadden, who volunteers at marriage prep classes in his local Catholic church. I will summarize what he said in the article but I urge you to read the whole article at Verily.com.[12] My comments are in parentheses.

When his marriage began to decline, as it does without effort, McFadden called three of his married friends and asked them how they avoided the declining marriage syndrome. Their responses: The first friend urged him to get over it; no one is happily married. The second said this is what happens in marriage: the initial passion fades, and you end up bickering for the rest of your lives. The third asserted the key to surviving marriage is to have low expectations—very low.

---

[12] Peter McFadden, "Three Daily Rituals That Stop Spouses from Taking Each Other for Granted," *Verily*, Jul 16, 2015, https://verilymag.com/2015/07/relationship-advice-keeping-marriage-strong-appreciating-your-spouse.

He refused to accept their cynical conclusions. He did some research in preparation to speak in a marriage prep class. He came up with three rituals to nourish his twelve-year marriage.

1. A reunion ritual. When he first sees his wife at the end of a day, he asks her to dance. And they dance. (Dancing is best but if dancing is too radical, at least a smile, a word of praise like "My bride!" and a warm five-second hug *every day* would qualify for second best.)

2. Set aside two minutes each day for undistracted communication with each other. McFadden began having breakfast with his wife. Only after breakfast does that two minutes begin. He pats his knee and invites his wife to sit on his lap and they share what their day will be like. (Lap-sitting or no lap-sitting, this is great, and while at least holding hands. Touching is important!)

3. An appreciation ritual daily. They thank each other throughout the day and once in bed at night they thank one another for the things that the other did for them that day, big and small. McFadden wrote,

> I had become so focused on my petty complaints about my wife that I had forgotten what a good wife she was. Our thank you ritual to end the day has helped us become much more tolerant of each other's failings.[13]

(A number of studies have shown that people who are thankful every day are less likely to be depressed, they sleep better, they reduce their stress, and are less inclined to be substance abusers.[14])

---

[13] Ibid.
[14] National Alliance on Mental Illness (NAMI) California, "The Impact of Gratitude on Mental Health," https://namica.org/blog/the-impact-of-gratitude-on-mental-health/.

All of these ways of sharing affection (and I am sure there are many other great ways) are quite important to fulfill the need for five positive interactions for every negative one, as recommended in Chapter III.[15]

WOMEN: ASK FOR WHAT YOU WANT!

When I mentioned romantic affection to a group of young women, one remarked, "Father, that's what we want. Are there any men who do this?"

"Not many, not yet," I answered. "You may have to train them."

Wives, tell your husbands what you like and don't like. If they're smart, they'll respond. One of my pre-seminary sweethearts said, "I love it when you touch my face." I'm not a rocket scientist, but I knew enough to keep touching her face in those special moments of sharing affection. Wives, it's not manipulation to ask for what you like; it's teaching a man how to treat you right. It's only manipulation if you try to *make* him do things he doesn't want to do. Persuasion, on the other hand, is getting him to want to do something new (for the sake of love).

Affection is an extremely important love language in marriage. It seems that many marriages are lacking in this, because it was seen only as a prelude to sex while dating. Not true. It is a beautiful language of love.

Affection, as Karol Wojtyła (Pope John Paul II) wrote in *Love and Responsibility*, is not aimed at enjoyment, "but the feeling of nearness." Sharing affection "has the power to deliver love from the various dangers implicit in the egoism of the senses...." Affection is an important "factor of love," but requires an "inner self-control."[16]

---

[15] Gottman, *Why Marriages Succeed or Fail*, 56–58.
[16] John Paul II, "Wednesday Address of November 5, 1980," in *Man and Woman He Created Them* (Boston, MA: Pauline Books and Media, 2006), 203.

Occasionally a person discovers his or her spouse has little use for affection; he/she has difficulty embracing or touching. Sometimes this reticence stems from the fact that he/she comes from a family where outward expressions of affection were rare. Another possibility is a psychological block due to a bad experience in the past. In either case, I would recommend discussing this delicately and diplomatically, and explaining the importance of trying to gradually ease into a habit of sharing affection as husband and wife. This is something that can be learned, but it must be done gradually, without any outside pressure.

In the case of a psychological block, for their own good, and that of their marriage and their children, they should consider getting some counseling to get at the root problem. Often such a problem can cause major difficulties with loving or trusting fully. Getting counseling from a skilled Christian counselor can be extremely beneficial.

To be sure, cultural background has a huge impact on the ability to share affection. Generally, Latins, Filipinos, and some Eastern Europeans are quite comfortable with hugging and kissing among family members and friends. This does not mean that those from other backgrounds should be satisfied with minimal affection. Many studies show that sharing affection physically is quite therapeutic for everyone, regardless of nationality.

It is also important to be affectionate with children. As Gary Smalley indicates in his excellent book for parents *The Blessing,* healthy touching at home can "protect a child from looking to meet this need [for affection] in all the wrong places."[17] Jesus himself had

---

[17] Gary Smalley, *The Blessing* (New York, NY: Pocket Books, 1990), 49.

the children come to him, "took them in his arms, laid his hands on them and blessed them" (Mk 10:16).

Smalley also points out that meaningful touch brings physiological benefits for couples, including lowering blood pressure, and can add almost two years to a husband's life.[18]

Some fathers do not hug or kiss their daughters once they become teenagers. Perhaps this is because as their daughters begin to develop into women, they feel it might be inappropriate to show them physical affection. Not so. It speaks volumes for a father to give his daughter a good chaste hug. Psychologists who have dealt with the sad consequences in daughters whose fathers did not hug them are united in encouraging this.

So, husbands, remember the importance of affection for your wives, and for your daughters and sons as well. With discretion and sensitivity, affection is a real plus at any age. It's a great aid for mental well-being and a great thing in marriage. It symbolizes and fosters intimacy without the likelihood of exploitation.

EROS (EMOTIONAL LOVE)

The fourth of the "four loves" (after agape, friendship, and affection) is emotional love, or *eros*. It means *to be well pleased by someone or something, to like very much*. We sometimes use love in this sense to describe our feelings about a new stereo, a new car or house: "I just love it!" What we really mean is that we *like* it a great deal, but somehow it doesn't suffice to say, "I like it very much!" "Love" in the English language has come to be a superlative of "like."

---

[18] Ibid., 46.

In marriage, emotional love means infatuation, the emotional attraction for another which seems, but is not, uncontrollable. It is usually at a peak on the day of the wedding. Pope John Paul II remarked in his talks on the theology of the body, "According to Plato, 'eros' represents the interior force that attracts man towards everything good, true, and beautiful...."[19] In our context, it means that strong desire for the good, the true, and the beautiful in the spouse. This is the strongest emotional feeling of attraction short of a mystical experience. It is being "in love."

Eros is not merely sexual desire as Freud mistakenly taught, although sexual attraction may play a part. It is primarily personal. One desire is to possess the whole person, not just the body. As such, it is far more powerful than sexual attraction.

What is the purpose of this love? Most likely it is designed to be a catalyst for marriage, helping couples overcome hesitancy in making the lifelong commitment of marriage.

In fact, it is perhaps the prime inducement to marry, although as lovers in Hollywood have proven time and again, not the prime ingredient for a successful marriage. I remember hearing an actress many years back, commenting on television about her fifth marriage. "This," she cooed, "is real love. The others [four!] were not. This marriage will last because our love is authentic." A few years later that marriage was on the rocks as well. She was thinking that a strong emotional attraction was "authentic" love. Not so. An authentic love is one that pursues energetically the good of the beloved (agape) and practices affection and friendship

---

[19] John Paul II, "Wednesday Address of November 5, 1980," in *Man and Woman He Created Them*, 316.

for the purpose of that love. Its reward is intimacy.

C. S. Lewis makes a point we would do well to remember: if you make a god out of eros it will become a demon and destroy you. Eros is a wonderful, marvelous thing, but it is only finite; it is not God. It apes God, insofar as it is so far above other earthly joys that it seems to be a god, but it is not. God alone is infinite, everlasting. Eros is neither.

When I was in the seminary, I heard the story of a woman who told a priest that she thought she was in love with him. When he calmly told her that such things can happen, she asked him how he could treat it so lightly. He gently explained to her that falling in love is not the end of the world. Emotions go where they will, but if you don't cultivate eros, it will fade in time. It did.

Every married person should be acutely aware of this fact. No married person is immune from falling in love with someone else. There are precautions one can take, but sometimes it just happens. If it does, a sober knowledge of its limits will protect a spouse from doing something terribly stupid (like running off with the object of that feeling).

If you know how finite this God-imitating love is, and realize you don't need to surrender to it whenever it pops up, you will avoid lots of misery. Nonetheless, when it is shared with your spouse and it is understood for what it is, it is very sweet.

Emotional love invariably fades in any relationship for two reasons. First, it thrives on mystery, and mystery fades with familiarity. Second, as a human love, it is limited and needs to be nourished and sustained by divine love. If it is not divinized, it will die as all things merely human must die.

How does one keep it alive—even if not at a wedding day high—in marriage? First, by growing and enriching oneself in virtue, holiness, and knowledge, thereby preserving some mystery in the relationship. Second, by practicing divine love (agape). In these ways, emotional love, good in itself, can be kept alive, and the relationship retains a certain pizzazz.

Emotional love can be expressed by words: "I'm in love with you," or actions. But by what actions? Passionate acts for passionate feelings? To extend this reasoning to other feelings would require angry acts for angry feelings (perhaps throwing a chair or two, or breaking a window), and jealous acts for jealous feelings (perhaps a punch in the mouth). Granted, feelings should be expressed, but in a constructive, reasonable way.

Passionate acts and their natural conclusion, sexual intercourse, signify something much deeper than a feeling. They symbolize commitment, exclusiveness, a total self-gift. They symbolize a love so rich that it wishes to bring forth new life with whom to share that love.

The most honest physical expression of emotional love is romantic affection. This way of touching, hugging, and kissing expresses a pure gratitude and delight in the happiness of this other who has brought such happiness to me. This is the Christian way of expressing eros, stripped of the selfishness that kills all love, and divinized by divine love. And it is this expression of eros that, because divinized, will enable it to last.

There is a danger in marriage that is analogous to the problem of sexual activity before marriage. It is the fact that hugging and gentle kissing, holding hands, cuddling, and other forms of affection are primarily about intimacy. Sexual activity is filled with pleasure, and can turn into self-gratification especially for the husband. It can become a very selfish thing.

To avoid this danger spouses must remember the Christian view of sex as expressed in *Gaudium et Spes*. Namely, that the conjugal act "signifies and fosters the mutual self-donation by which spouses enrich each other with a joyful and a ready mind."[20] What this often means in practice is that the man adapts his sexual activity to the tempo of the woman, thereby manifesting a truly self-giving concern for her fulfillment in the act.

We will speak more of this under "Christian Sex," but in a nutshell, a woman is like an iron, and a man like a match. That is, a woman is slow to warm up to having marital intimacy, a man almost instantaneous. So he must take plenty of time to warm her up by touching, embracing, etc., holding off on what he might be inclined to do right away. Then, after completion, he should attend to her, despite the fact that the match has gone out, to help her descend gently. The husband who practices this will most likely have twice as much sex as the one who simply follows his natural instincts selfishly. And he'll have a good deal more intimacy.

In the Eucharist we find the promise of fulfillment of the natural impulse of emotional love: the consummation of the beloved. In receiving the Eucharist, we consume our God as he consumes us more and more into his life of grace, as a sign of the all-consuming love that awaits us in his Kingdom. Emotional love, then, is a sign of the overwhelming fire with which our entire being will burn at the mere sight of God,

---

[20] *Gaudium et Spes*, n. 49.

who created in his own image the creatures for whom
our hearts burn in this world.

Incidentally, the word eros does not appear in the
Bible. But the Song of Songs is full of eros; it is the
story of a passionate love between God and his people:

> You have ravished my heart, my sister, my bride;
> you have ravished my heart with one glance
>   of your eyes,
> with one bead of your necklace.
> How beautiful is your love, my sister, my bride,
> how much more delightful is your love than
>   wine,
> and the fragrance of your ointments than all
>   spices!
> Your lips drip honey, my bride,
> sweetmeats and milk are under your tongue;
> And the fragrance of your garments
> is the fragrance of Lebanon.
> You are an enclosed garden, my sister, my bride,
> an enclosed garden, a fountain sealed.
> You are a park that puts forth pomegranates,
> with all choice fruits. (Song of Sg 4:9–12)

And, moreover, we can all develop a passionate love
for God here on earth. Although this is a concept foreign to most Christians, St. Augustine expressed it well:

> Late have I loved you, O Beauty so ancient and
> so new. I rushed headlong after these things of
> beauty which you made. They kept me far from
> you, those fair things which, were they not in
> you, would not exist at all. You have sent forth
> fragrance, and I have drawn in my breath, and
> I pant for you. I have tasted you, and I hunger
> and thirst for you. You have touched me and
> I have burned for your peace.[21]

---

[21] St. Augustine of Hippo, *The Confessions of St. Augustine*, trans.
John K. Ryan (New York: Image Books, 1960), 254–55.

SUMMARY

Each of the four types of love has its own place in a marriage. All four are good in their right place. Only agape is divine, and gives life to all the others. The three human loves wither and die in selfishness if they are not animated by divine love. If agape becomes, by grace, the pervasive theme of your life, two things will happen. First, you will begin to love as God loves, something you—and your spouse—will delight to see. Second, you will be able to unite in love with God and others. No other earthly delight can exceed that of good relationships. Nothing else will bring lasting happiness in courtship, in marriage, or in heaven.

CHAPTER V

Husbands, Love Your Wives

"HUSBANDS, LOVE YOUR WIVES, AS Christ loved the church and gave himself up for her.... Let each one of you love his wife as himself" (Eph 5:25, 33). The Scriptures encourage husbands to love their wives in more than one passage (three times in Ephesians 5). Another passage is from Colossians: "Husbands, love your wives, and do not be harsh with them" (3:19). Verse 33 of Ephesians 5 has an instruction for women as to how to treat their husbands, but that is the subject of the next chapter. Always the verb used is the Greek *agapao*, namely, the unconditional self-giving which imitates divine love.

Men should be very clear with themselves as to what they vowed on their wedding day. "I promise to be true to you in good times and bad, in sickness and health. I will love you and honor you all the days of my life." This is an *unconditional* love. It means that he will work for his spouse's good no matter what—in good times and bad. So, if she is mean and nasty toward him, he will still work for her good. If she does terrible things, he will still be willing to serve her and help her find happiness. I wonder if most men realize that this is what they vowed on their wedding day. It's quite a noble and beautiful commitment. And it usually works wonders to keep a marriage intact.

Only in Titus 2:4 does Scripture speak of women loving their husbands, exhorting the older women to "be reverent" so they can teach the younger women to "love their husbands and children." Why do the Scriptures encourage only the husbands to love their wives? I would suggest that it's because women, being heart-connected, tend to be good at loving; men must work at it. Of course it is good work, but it is harder in general (with some rare exceptions to be sure) for men to love their wives than vice versa. Of course, the million-dollar question is "How do they do that?"

To love someone—anyone—a person must discover what the beloved wants, what they like. The man who loves his wife by giving her what *he* likes or wants is usually not successful. This is because her wants are often quite different from his.

DISCOVERING WHAT SHE WANTS

Gary Smalley suggests that most men figure they know how to please their wives, but alas, they don't. Smalley himself learned that the hard way when he surprised his wife by having their house painted. She appreciated his effort but she would have much preferred to have the kitchen floor replaced.

Thankfully, he wasn't stupid. He put on hold all the projects he had in mind and got the kitchen floor replaced. Then, he sat down and made a list of *her* priorities. It was quite a different list than what he had in mind, but he was learning. If you want to please your wife, don't give her what you want her to have. Give her what she really wants![1]

How does a husband know what his wife wants? *He asks her!* And as we mentioned above, she needs

---

[1] Gary Smalley, *If Only He Knew: What No Woman Can Resist* (Grand Rapids: Zondervan, 1998), 27–28.

to tell him what she wants. That may sound simple, but it isn't. Men want to think they know what their wives want and women think that men should know. Both are wrong. He needs to ask, and she needs to tell him even if he doesn't.

AFFECTION

Willard Harley, in his best-selling *His Needs, Her Needs*, claims the first thing a woman wants is affection. With most women on this planet, I think he is right on target.

He tells the story of a woman who married the man of her dreams. After several months, however, a real problem arose. Whenever she would be affectionate with him, he would get aroused and expect to have sex. It turns out that her husband's mother died when he was just ten and he was raised by his father and two brothers. There was little affection before his mother died, and just about none thereafter. He didn't know how to be affectionate without moving into sex.

His wife met a man at work who was quite affectionate, with her and everyone else. She came to crave that affection. In time she fell into an adulterous affair with the man.

Harley points out that virtually all women have a great need for affection, especially hugs. Hugs and holding hands can be a great warmer for any marriage relationship.

I was discussing affection with a group of our married women, most of whom were daily communicants, saying how important it is to share this with their husbands. A couple of them said, "Oh no, Father. When they get affectionate with us we push them off because it means they want to have sex."

"What an impoverishment," I responded. "Affection is such a beautiful expression of love, of intimacy. How sad that it has been co-opted into sex."

Now, some husbands will respond to their wives' requests for affection without sex with "I'm not the affectionate type. And I'm not going to start now!"[2] That is a perfect recipe for disaster.

Men can learn to be affectionate. I learned it when some of our youth group members wanted to hug Father. It was a bit new for me, but I quickly realized how important it was for them. For some it was a healing thing.

Harley has a list of things a husband can do to show affection toward his wife. Some items from that list are as follows:

1. Hug and kiss your wife every morning while you are still in bed.
2. Tell her you love her over breakfast.
3. Kiss her before you leave for work.
4. Remember to give gifts for special occasions (birthday, anniversary, etc.). Put a reminder on your phone!
5. Hug and kiss her when you get home. Ask how her day went.
6. Hug and kiss her every night before bed.[3]

Some marriage writers or speakers suggest that men practice affection so they will get more sex. Well, it is true that a man will probably have more sex if he gives more affection, but that is too utilitarian a motive. The prime motive for a man to give affection is to make

---

[2] Willard F. Harley Jr., *His Needs, Her Needs* (Grand Rapids: Revell 2022), 34.
[3] Ibid., 37–38.

his wife happy, to fulfill his marriage vows. "... I will love and honor you all the days of my life." It is this sort of love and the intimacy that follows that will fulfill *him* as a person.

THE AFFECTION-SHY WIFE

What if the wife is not big on affection and he is? This, of course, is not the norm but it can happen. I actually worked with a couple like this. He had a Latin background and she did not. I encouraged her to try to learn little by little to be more affectionate. If a man can learn to be affectionate, a woman certainly can.

The exception to that rule would be if a woman was abused or traumatized by way of physical touch. If that is the case, she would probably benefit from some counseling to help her to trust her husband in the sharing of affection.

Marriage writers Patricia Love and Steven Stosny suggest that fear is a very important factor for a woman in marriage. A woman fears being alone: alone at home; or alone in her life goals, such as a loving family, a peaceful home, and a romantic spouse, among other things.[4] Think of how a husband's show of affection every day could allay those fears.

THE FIVE LOVE LANGUAGES

All of this talk of a man satisfying his wife's need for affection calls to mind the issue of the five love languages, beautifully expounded upon by Gary Chapman. He identifies five different love "languages" that individual persons may prefer. The key to having a

---

[4] Patricia Love and Steven Stosny, *How to Improve Your Marriage Without Talking About It* (New York: Broadway Books 2007), 72–74.

successful marriage, says Chapman, is to discover the primary love language of your spouse and to pursue that first and foremost.

The love languages he identifies are as follows:

1. Affirming Words
2. Quality Time
3. Receiving Gifts
4. Acts of Service
5. Physical Touch[5]

Couples often have problems because they do things for their spouse based on what *they would like*, not realizing that their spouse very likely has a different "primary love language." So it's essential to know your primary love language and that of the other. And you should manifest love mostly in the other's language, not your own.

According to a survey done by blogger Matt Zajechowski, quality time is the favorite US love language to receive. But "acts of service" is the favorite love language to give. Receiving gifts rates lowest for both giving and receiving.[6]

WORDS OF AFFIRMATION

Although it's important to "speak" the partner's primary love language a good deal, all the love languages should be spoken. It seems that the need for affirmation is behind the idea of having Mother's Day every May. That is a day when it is clearly expected that husband and children show Mom how much she

---

[5] Gary Chapman, *The Five Love Languages* (Chicago: Northfield Publishing, 2004).
[6] Matt Zajechowski, "The most popular love language in each U. S. state," Preply, updated May 22, 2024, https://preply.com/en/blog/most-popular-love-languages/.

is appreciated. (We will consider the love languages for men to speak in the next section.) The man who often praises his wife for the things she does (and who seldom complains about what she does not do) will build her confidence level and inspire her to keep going. Every right-minded man wants a self-confident wife, not a mouse.

The husband who tells his wife every day, "I love you" will reap great rewards, as will telling her why he loves her. The husband who complains to his wife every day will soon reap misery. No doubt, that is why just about every marriage counselor urges couples to stop criticizing. As mentioned previously, the couple that put into effect the "two praises for every criticism" reaped bounteous rewards in their marriage. Every husband should make a list of all the good things about his wife, and then mention one or two every day.

QUALITY TIME

One young wife told me how difficult their marriage had been of late. I asked her if she ever took time out to sit and talk to her husband or go out on a date. She replied, "Oh no. We're too busy." I warned her that if they are too busy to spend quality time together, they are just asking for trouble.

As we mentioned regarding communication (in an earlier anecdote), the husband who takes the time to listen to his wife for a good chunk of time every day is going to be very happy with the results. Why don't men listen like this? Because they feel their wife gives three times the detail necessary to get the story told, and they get antsy partway through. And in most cases their wife *does* give three times the necessary detail. *But* this is an excellent investment of time on his part. The man who listens carefully to his wife's (many) words and tries hard to understand her message is providing her great therapy and building a beautiful relationship.

Of course, one way to do this is to go on dates, as we mentioned previously. Perhaps that's why so many books on marriage insist on couples having lots of dates. And, of course, men should be happy to know that when they listen to their wife, they need not fix her. Just listen. No newspapers, no TV, no computer, no other distractions. Just man and wife listening and talking.

In one of his radio programs John Gray tells of a date he went on with his wife some years back. His wife had been urging him to take her to the opera for months, and since he didn't like opera, he carefully avoided the subject. Finally, one day, he decided he really should bite the bullet and take her out to the opera. Off they went and she was delighted. According to the story he told, when they drove the car into the garage, she couldn't resist him. They renewed their marriage covenant right there in the car (if you know what I mean). He couldn't believe it!

The next day she heard John making a phone call, asking to purchase season tickets to the opera. Intelligent man.

GIFTS

Although gifts may not be high on the list of favorite love languages, gift-giving is still important. The key to gift-giving is to give something your wife really wants or needs. And it helps if it has a romantic aspect to it. A rose, or a dozen roses, or her favorite candy is likely to be a much bigger hit than a new trash can or toaster. However, if you are going to be a good gift-giver, you need to do some research. Listen carefully to your wife and take notes on the things she really wants.

And the gift of a card can be just the right thing at times. In fact, one of the very good books on marriage is *Letters from Dad* by Greg Vaughn. He wanted to give his wife and children some good memories so he decided he would write them letters—love letters.

He called together some friends and they brainstormed the letters project. They were all to write letters expressing unconditional love to their wives without any criticisms.

After a few weeks the results of their adventure began to trickle in. They were very good. One of the men had written his letter on green striped stationery, and since he was unable to find a fancy box, he used some old box, hardly a class act. Nonetheless, he said it was the best thing ever to happen in his twenty-five-year marriage. He gave it to her at an anniversary party, with lots of family present, and after she read it, she cried. When he offered to read it out loud, she could hardly hold back the tears long enough to whisper "Yes." When he did, she was thrilled.

Another man read it to his wife over dinner and through her tears she kissed him and thanked him repeatedly. Yet another gave it to his wife on the couch and she cried so much she couldn't finish it. She had him finish it, and both cried so much he had to change his shirt.

One man surprised her with a rose-decorated hotel room complete with candlelight and champagne. The elegantly wrapped box with the letter was on the bed.

She proclaimed that "it was the greatest treasure of her life." All had similar stories.

The prizewinner was the man who took his wife to her favorite restaurant and gave his magnificently boxed letter to the maître d' to hold until the right time. He asked what was in it and the man told him, "A letter, telling her how much I love her." The hostess overheard this and said, "Oh, that's so sweet."

By the time he went to retrieve the box, half the restaurant staff had been tipped off, and they followed him to the table as he prepared to present it to his wife. She looked up at the small crowd gathered and asked, "Why are you doing this?"

"Because I love you," was his ready reply, bringing an "Ahhhh" from everyone in the place.

She read the letter and spoke from her heart, "To know you took the time to do all this . . . and to do so without fear, without shame, and without worrying what anyone else thought—I just want you to know from my heart, I will treasure this forever. You have made an imprint on my life that will never wash away."[7]

Whoa!

Why did these men have to write letters? Why couldn't they just *say* what they were thinking? Because it should take a bit of time to prepare such a letter, and it may take some editing by a friend. And, of course, letters last. The wives who got these letters saved them and went back to look at them from time to time. They were treasured, as were the husbands who composed them. Now there is a gift that works!

---

[7] This section is based on Greg Vaughn, *Letters from Dad* (Nashville: Integrity Publishers, 2005), 44–48.

ACTS OF SERVICE

Does taking the garbage out or putting the dishes away from the dishwasher count as saying "I love you"? Of course! Often wives tell me that it is very hard to get their husbands to do anything around the house. I recommend, as do many marriage writers, that they put up a board entitled "honey-do list." They write on it things they would like done, and perhaps add a number for the priority they give to each task. Every husband should see such a list as a wonderful way to live out his marriage vows and to fulfill the second great commandment of love ("love your neighbor as yourself"). There are scores of things a man can do for his wife but those on the honey-do list are some of the most important.

As for the love language of physical touch, we spoke of it above, under "Affection." Physical touch without any ulterior motives. Just touches to express and facilitate personal (not merely sexual) intimacy. Very important!

FOR HUSBANDS: A CURE FOR THE WIFELY HEADACHE

"Father, my wife has a *lot* of headaches. What can I do? I feel so rejected when she doesn't want to have relations with me."

"Are you willing to be a little bit humble to warm her up?"

"Do I have to?"

"Only if you want to have more marital relations with her and a happy marriage."

"Okay, Father. I'll try anything."

"For starters, I want you to think of any harsh words you have said to your wife in the last month, any ways you may have hurt her. Can you think of any?"

[Pause] "Yeah, I can think of one or two. But she deserved it. She..."

"Forget it. Do you want to die a lonely, divorced man?"

"No, but you should know what she..."

"That's immaterial. Do you want a loving, warm, intimate, passionate wife?"

"That would be nice..."

"Then stop trying to accuse your wife and defend yourself. Here's what you do. Tonight, when you're in bed, look over at your wife and say, 'I've hurt you a lot lately, haven't I?' She'll say, perhaps rather coldly, 'Yes.' You say, 'Look, I'm sorry. I'm really sorry. I forget how to be sensitive sometimes. I've been all worried about myself and haven't considered your feelings. I really want to make amends.'

"She may not trust you yet. She may say something like, 'You've said that before.'

"Now you've got to show her you mean business. 'Okay, I deserved that. But I really want to try. I need your help. Tell me one thing I can do to begin to start to heal things.'

"'Okay,' she says, still coldly. 'Don't ever get angry at me in front of the children.'

"'All right. I'll work at it. I'm really sorry I did that to you. I may not be able to reform overnight, but the next time I do that I'll give myself a penance of one decade of the rosary and I'll pay you twenty bucks.'

"'I want an escrow fund,' she says with a faint smile, starting to warm a bit.

"'You've got it. Tomorrow morning, I'll put sixty bucks in the bureau. Hopefully, I won't need all of it.'

"'That would be nice,' she answers, still a bit cautious about the new you."

"Well, Father, when are we going to have relations?"

"Not tonight. Tell her you love her and go to sleep."

"C'mon, Father. I thought you were going to get things straight for us. Now I have to wait another night?"

"Don't think in terms of nights. Maybe weeks. Look, there's a lot to fix here. Be patient."

"So what do I do next?"

"You begin to work on fulfilling your promise. After a week, you call her on the phone. Call her Monday morning."

"And?"

"And you ask her out for a date."

"Okay."

"What are you going to say?"

"Hi, hon', let's go to a movie Saturday."

"That won't do."

"What's wrong with that?"

"No wonder you're having problems. You can't ask a woman out on a date like that."

"She's no woman. She's my wife!"

"She's a woman and you have to make her feel special. You call her up and say 'Hello, Mrs. Snodgrass. This is a secret admirer. Would you consider having dinner with me this Saturday at the Escargot?'"

"Wait a second, Father, that's an expensive restaurant. What's wrong with a movie?"

"You can afford it. Movies are no good. You don't talk. Women like to talk."

"Okay, so we go out to dinner. Then what?"

"Then dancing."

"Okay, then we come home, right?"

"Yup."

"And then...?"

"Sorry Charlie ... er, Melvin. You have a way to go. You bring her to the door and say, 'May I kiss you goodnight?'"

"I have to ask her for a kiss?"

"She'll like it. Treat her like your prom date."

"And if she says yes?"

"Then you give her the slowest, gentlest, most tender kiss you've ever given her. And, you give her a big long, tender hug, and say, 'I'm so glad I married you.'"

"And then, Father, and then ... "

"Calm down, buddy. You might have a little something to eat and then you go to bed."

"But Father, what about ... "

"Don't say a word about that. Just be very sweet and see what develops. If nothing happens that night, don't worry. This takes time. You have a lot of healing to do. You want to rekindle her trust. If you do that, you may be able to get rid of your electric blanket someday."

"Are you sure this will work, Father?"

"Trust me. What choice do you have?"

"None."

"Women don't want to have sex with a man. They want to have sex with their lover. You haven't been her lover in quite a while. And, if you begin to love her, you'll have a lot more than good sex."

"Father, I *love* my wife. I bought her a refrigerator last year. I got her a brand-new minivan this year ... "

"You're a regular Casanova, aren't you? Look, Melvin, those things are good, they help. But a woman needs a lot more than refrigerators and minivans to feel loved."

"Like what?"

"Remember three key things about loving a woman. First, she is *very* connected to her heart. You must nourish her heart at all times. Never yell, never say anything hurtful, and often hold her and tell her you're there for her, especially when she's blue. In fact, at least one twenty-second hug each day would do wonders. Give her lots of good, honest compliments. Always honor her, as you promised you would on your wedding day. Second, remember that most women like to talk. You have to spend time talking to her, and especially *listening* to her. And, third, women like a little pizzazz in their lives. You and I do just fine with three meals a day, doing our work, and watching the ball game on Sunday. Not women. They need a little fun, a trip to New York, a week in the Virgin Islands, or a night at the opera. Give her a little color. Most women love these things, and you'll enjoy them too."

"That's it?"

"Those are the basics. You may have to make some refinements along the way. You can ask her to coach you if you like. And, you have to make all this a habit, and do it because you want to make *her* happy, not just to improve your sex life."

"Actually, Father, this sounds pretty good. She's said almost as much to me before, but I have a terrible memory."

"Most of us do. Write it down! And remember, if you nourish the heart of your wife, she'll make you a happy man for life. And, far less importantly, you'll save hundreds of dollars on Advil!"

NOTHING'S WRONG

A brief word here about dealing with an unhappy wife. If a man senses that something is wrong with his wife or with their relationship, he usually asks her, "Is something wrong? Did I do something wrong?" If she answers "Nothing," she does *not* want him to go back to reading the sports page. When a man says, "Nothing's wrong," he usually means, well . . . nothing's wrong. When a woman says that with a sad expression, it usually means that there is plenty wrong!

He needs to gently prod her as Gary Smalley prodded his wife when she refused to tell him that she was tired of being in second place behind almost every other activity. He did well to persevere in his inquiry, and his perseverance yielded good results.

SUMMARY

For a husband to love his wife means to always work for her good, for her happiness. And the marriage vows call for him to do this noble work "in good times and bad." In other words, he must love his wife *unconditionally*. This is something he should meditate on a great deal, and do daily.

A husband must ask his wife what is important to her and what makes her happy. One thing that pleases just about every woman is for a husband to be affectionate, without expecting his affection to lead to sexual intimacy. Lots of hugs should be on every husband's list of things to do. Although he should emphasize his wife's favorite "love language," he should speak all five of these languages to his wife. One thing that many wives seem to like is for a husband to write her a beautiful love letter from time to time. It is hard to overemphasize the importance of this for a happy marriage.

Even though loving your wife will probably lead to more marital sex, if that is your only motive, you'll be in trouble. With your wife . . . and with God. You're supposed to love your wife because you vowed to love her regardless of how much sex you have ("in good times and bad"), and because Christians are supposed to love their neighbors. You wife should be your preeminent neighbor. And, of course, love is what fulfills us as persons.

The husbands who do these things are usually *very* happy people. Remember, your wife is the heart of the home. If your wife is happy, the whole family will be happy.

CHAPTER VI

The Precious Wife

A good wife who can find?
She is far more precious than jewels.
The heart of her husband trusts in her,
and he will have no lack of gain.
She does him good, and not harm,
all the days of her life. (Proverbs 31:10–12)

R-E-S-P-E-C-T

As will the husband who wants to stay married, the "precious" wife will be very attuned to what her spouse wants. An excellent clue as to what he wants (in addition to sexual intimacy) is found in Ephesians 5:32: "... let each one of you love his wife as himself, and let the wife see that she respects her husband." Emerson Eggerichs has taken this short passage from Ephesians and elaborated on it. He states, "men are commanded to love because they don't love naturally, and on the other side, women are commanded to respect because they don't respect naturally."[1]

He repeats what most have heard before about loving your spouse unconditionally, but he adds, based on this quote from Ephesians, that a wife should *respect* her husband unconditionally. Yes, he proposes that wives *respect* their husbands no matter what.

Now some wives say, "Well, he has to earn my respect." There is some respect that must be earned. A baseball batter, a brokerage firm, a law firm, an ice

---

[1] Emerson Eggerichs, *Love and Respect* (Nashville: Thomas A. Nelson Publishers 2004), 70.

cream producer. All of these must earn respect. No one is going to respect them just because they are there.

But as Christians we should respect each and every person. Why? Because they are created in the image and likeness of God, and they have been invited to live in the Kingdom of God. It's just something we do, not because they are good, but because *we* are good. Sometimes the respect a Christian gives a person who is struggling is just what they need to turn things around.

A wife has an even more important reason to respect her husband. Just about every wife promises to do this on her wedding day: "I will love you and *honor* you all the days of my life." To honor your husband is to respect him.

Eggerichs reports on a survey of 400 men who were asked to choose between two unpleasant options: (a) "to be left alone and unloved in the world" or (b) "to feel inadequate and disrespected by everyone." Seventy-four percent preferred (a) to be left alone and unloved. Many husbands told Eggerichs that they would rather their wife respect them without love than vice versa.[2]

Eggerichs mentions another survey taken by Decision Analysts, Inc. regarding a conflict situation in marriage. The men were to choose between the following two options when they were in the midst of an argument:

> (a) That my wife doesn't respect me right now, or (b) That my wife doesn't love me right now.
>
> Eighty-one percent answered (a) . . . no respect.[3]

In the movie *Fireproof* (one of the best ever on marriage, in my opinion) the husband complains that his

---

[2] Ibid., 49.
[3] Ibid., 58.

wife did not *respect* him. Indeed, she didn't, and he didn't love her as he should have. When he started loving and she started respecting, the marriage was saved.

Marriage expert Steven Stosny says something similar about the needs of men. He writes, "A man's greatest pain comes from shame due to the inadequacy he feels in relationships; therefore, going to the relationship for comfort is like seeking solace from the enemy."[4] Feeling shame is the antithesis of feeling respected. This is why men are reticent to ask for directions when they are driving, and why they so often delay making doctor's appointments. They don't want to appear vulnerable.

The Scriptures seem to corroborate this. The word "shame" appears 177 times in the Bible. Twenty-nine of those are in the Psalms. Many of these involve a curse upon evil-doers with statements like, "Let them be put to shame and confusion who seek my life! Let them be turned back and brought to dishonor who desire my hurt!" (Ps 70:2); and "Let [God's enemies] be put to shame and dismayed forever; let them perish in disgrace" (83:17); and "May all who hate Zion be put to shame and turned backward!" (129:5).

How do wives shame their husbands? When there is an argument, she may attack him because he does not do what she thinks he should do. He interprets this as her not respecting him. Her heart rate does not increase much in an argument, but his does. He feels uncomfortable and he tends to want to withdraw from this conversation. When he withdraws, she feels she needs to turn up the heat so she gets nasty to get his attention. She may even start bringing up old issues.

---

[4] Love and Stosny, *How to Improve Your Marriage*, 16.

That causes him to withdraw even further and World War III ensues.[5]

There are many ways to please a husband but most of them are bound up with respect.

ACCEPTANCE

One woman whose wedding I was scheduled to officiate was being prepared by her local priest for the sacrament. He asked her at one point if there were any shortcomings in her husband that bothered her. She answered, "He had a lot of faults, but I fixed them all." As the subsequent years proved, there were still a few faults to deal with.

Many women try so hard to change their husbands, and the more they try, the more the husbands resist. Men don't like being manipulated. One classic example of this is when wives try to get their husbands to attend Mass or other religious devotions. Anything more than gently inviting him to attend a religious event, or saying "I would love it if sometimes we could pray together" (without asking for a reply), can be very dangerous. I have seen many a husband get totally turned off to religious activities by a wife who pushed too hard.

When a wife—or any family member, for that matter—complains about their husband or son or daughter or parent not wanting to practice the faith, I urge them, "Let them be. We need to honor their freedom." The best way to get another family member to practice our faith is to become a saint. Then they may see what religion can do for a person.

One woman discovered a way to get her non-Catholic husband to join her for Sunday Mass. Her

5 Gottman, *Why Marriages Succeed or Fail*, 151–53.

pastor suggested she dress up and make an effort to look good every time she came to Mass. "Why should I do that?" she asked.

"Because a man likes to be with his wife when she looks her best," he replied.

So she made sure to look good for every Sunday Mass. Her husband began to join her.

This advice applies not only to Sunday Mass, but to other times as well. A woman would reap nice benefits if she often had her hair looking nice, if she wore a bit of lipstick and a touch of eye makeup as well. Men are said to be several times more visual than women and this is simply a way to accommodate the male nature.

I heard of one woman who would take a shower every afternoon at 4:30 p.m. to prepare for her husband's arrival at 5. Her husband was a happy man and her marriage lasted until death.

Of course, there are some women for whom their husbands are only too ready to change, or at least are open to it. How do they do it? By accepting their husbands and not trying to force them to change. This is quite a paradox, but it's true.

I had a pastor once—an Irish pastor—who could be very reluctant to do whatever I might suggest. The priest who had preceded me in that parish told me he had pleaded with him to install a fence for the baseball field so the balls would not roll into the woods all the time. The pastor would not budge. So I tried a different approach. When we started a softball league in the parish, I made sure never to mention the fence—not even once. One day, a parishioner said to him, "Father, the softball league is going great. Do you suppose we could get a fence to keep the balls from rolling into the woods?"

"Sure," answered the pastor. "How much will it cost? Five thousand, six?" The fence went in.

Of course, there are some things that a wife *must* speak up about, such as his making a dishonest deal, or substance abuse, or mistreating the children. If he is abusive to his wife, she needs to tell him later something like, "That wasn't like you. I was so surprised to hear that from you." Laura Doyle, in her bestselling book *The Surrendered Wife*, suggests a wife respond to an insulting or nasty comment with the single word, "Ouch," and then walk away.[6] Brilliant.

PRAISE AND ADMIRE HIM

One woman felt her husband was boring whenever he conversed with guests. He would speak in a very low tone, with long pauses between sentences. Those present would either interject their thoughts or try to change the subject. His wife would often jump in and finish the story for him. Once she read about how to praise and respect her husband, she changed her tactics. When he began to speak, she would give him her complete attention. This had the effect of forcing others at the table to listen to him. For several months he would speak directly to his wife because she seemed so interested in what he was saying. After she continued this behavior for some time, he began to develop more self-confidence. He became a more interesting conversationalist. Friends told his wife, "I could listen to your husband for hours."[7]

---

[6] Laura Doyle, *The Surrendered Wife*, 179.
[7] Helen Andelin, *Fascinating Womanhood* (New York: Bantam Books, 1990), 81. (Out of print but now available as free PDF download at https://archive.org/details/fascinating-womanhood-helen-andelin-updated-1990--annas-archive--libgenrs-nf-2155503/page/n7/mode/2up.)

Some women consider it their "duty" to criticize their prideful husbands. But that is not their proper role. The world will do a good job of bringing a proud man down to earth. His wife need not do that. In fact, it should be her goal to build him up, pride or no pride. She is the one person who should always be there to support and praise him. And if she is, she will foster the kind of intimacy which will make both her and her husband very happy.[8]

This does not mean she should lie or make up things to praise him for. But her goal should always be to see the good side of him and express her admiration of that. Just about every man has some good qualities. His wife must have seen those when she married him. Otherwise, she wouldn't have.

One woman told me she was struggling with her marriage. I asked her if she ever praised her husband. She said hardly ever. She was very free in her criticisms, and he had many faults (what man doesn't?). I encouraged her to go home and make a list of his good points and mention two or three of these every day. When I spoke to her six weeks later, she told me things were going much better.

Marriage counselor Gary Neuman's book *The Truth about Cheating* contains a section heading, "The Number One Mistake Wives Make: If I Appreciate Him He'll Never Change."[9] He points out that criticizing a husband does not motivate him; appreciation does. From what I have seen, the man whose wife praises him for his hard work, or taking care of the car, or playing with the children, will often say to himself,

---

[8] Andelin, *Fascinating Womanhood*, 144–45.
[9] M. Gary Neuman, *The Truth about Cheating: Why Men Stray and What You Can Do to Prevent It* (Hoboken: John Wiley & Sons, 2008), 66.

"I'll do even better: I'll take out the garbage" (which he hasn't done for several weeks).

One wife told me she did not want to have to thank her husband for doing things he is supposed to do. She ended up divorced. Another woman who was struggling in her marriage told me she began to thank her husband for everything—for putting gas in the car when they were out, for giving her grocery money, and so forth. She saved her marriage.

One woman stopped criticizing her husband and began to appreciate all he did for her and the family. She asked forgiveness for her constant complaining and proclaimed her love for him. He started doing all sorts of things for her. He finally agreed to lead family devotions after dinner after many years of refusing. He began making plans for all sorts of activities for him and his wife to do, and he took over the bill-paying. He began to build her a set of shelves, and other such things. The more admiration she gave him, the more things he dreamed up to do for her.[10]

A number of marriage books recommend that wives who stay at home to raise their children give the husband twenty or thirty minutes when he gets home to just relax without doing anything. After greeting the children, invite him to sit in his easy chair alone and just gaze into space. Men love this. After this decompression time the husband joins in the family activities.

One woman sat in my office and told me, "I'm so glad you give out *Fascinating Womanhood* in your marriage preparation classes. I have been carrying out just about everything in that book and my husband can't do

---

[10] Helen Andelin, *Fascinating Womanhood*, 70.

enough for me. He is always trying to find something more to do for me."

Although it is usually the men who have to learn to listen to their wives, the wives sometimes need help in this area as well.

UNDERMINING HIS AUTHORITY

A great way to alienate your husband is to undermine his authority. Sometimes this takes a subtle form, but the result is usually the same. The husband gets very angry inside, even if sometimes he does not know why.

As an example, suppose the couple have guests over for dinner. At one point the husband may say to the children, "It's almost nine o'clock; you should get ready for bed now." Suppose the wife disagrees, and she says, "I think, since we have guests, we could let them stay up later." Not good. What should she say to convey the same message without undermining his authority? How about this: "Do you suppose we could let them stay up later tonight since we have guests?"

One wife told me she thought one of her children needed to take a test to see if she had ADHD. The husband was dead set against it. She said to me, "I think I should just take her and get it done."

I answered, "I don't think that's a good idea."

"But I am absolutely sure she needs it. My husband is just being unreasonable," she countered.

"You may be absolutely right, but if you go off and do that against his wishes, you are asking for trouble, big trouble."

"So, what do you think I should do?" she asked.

"If I were you I would tell him, 'I really think she should be tested, and it could help her a lot. But, if you don't want it to happen, I will go along with your wishes.'"

She was not so happy with this solution, and it was clear that she had not followed this pattern in the past. That is why, I suspect, her marriage was on the ropes, and why she had come for counseling. I asked her, "What would you rather have, a daughter who had been diagnosed for a problem and a divorce, or an untested daughter and an improving marriage?"

She went for option two. Some months later her marriage had improved dramatically. This, of course, was not just because she gave in on this one point, but because she learned thereafter to give in when he was strongly opposed to other ideas.

Laura Doyle had a classic exchange with her husband before she became a "surrendered wife."

> Him: The brakes are starting to go on the car, so I'm gonna take it in next week.
>
> Her: Next week? Brakes are pretty serious, John. Don't you think you should take it in right away?...
>
> Him: I don't have time right away. The brakes are good enough to last another week.
>
> Her: Hmm. I think you should take it in right away. Why wait until next week?
>
> Him: I'm not going to have time right now.
>
> Her: You need to make time for things like that.
>
> Him: There's just too much going on and it has to be next week.
>
> Her: So are you going to take it in?
>
> Him: Next week!

> Her: Maybe I can take it in for you.

> Him: Why don't you just put my head under
> the wheel and drive over it!

Laura writes what her new, non-controlling
approach would have been:

> Him: The brakes are starting to go on the car,
> so I'm gonna take it in next week.

> Her: Thank you for taking care of that.[11]

"Along this path of respect, you will find peace,
relief, joy, and passion that you will never find any
other way."[12] And, as Ms. Doyle says throughout the
book, you will find intimacy. Her point is that the
feminist notion that men are stupid and cannot do
anything right is not only mistaken, but very coun-
terproductive. It is true that husbands make mistakes,
but once his wife gives back control, he will learn not
to make those mistakes, and husband and wife will
be close again.

Helen Andelin tells the story of her family vacation
in the Florida Keys. They were just beginning this
special time that they had anticipated for months. The
father called their son who was doing mission work
in Sweden. When he got off the phone, the father
announced they were going to have to go back home.
"He's not well and they are sending him home." Helen
believed it would be better to have him return to Florida so they could all have a relaxing time together. She
tried hard to convince her husband. Of course, she was
right! But when he insisted, and turned down all her
appeals, she went along with him.

[11] Laura Doyle, *The Surrendered Wife*, 60–61.
[12] Ibid., 62.

Years later, she overheard her children proclaiming that they never wanted to disobey their father. She asked them why not. They answered, "You were the key, Mom, because you always obeyed Dad, even when it was difficult." It was her example that deterred them from being rebellious children.[13]

GETTING HIM TO CLEAR OUT THE GARAGE (OR ANYTHING ELSE)

I hear from women quite often, "Father, how do I get my husband to do the things I need, without nagging him?" Excellent question. Many women seem to think that if they get mean and nasty he'll do what she wants. They are very mistaken, as experience shows.

The first thing to understand (as we mentioned in the chapter on communication) is that very few men do what their wives ask if they ask only once. It's just the nature of things. Most men require several requests before they respond, and wives should realize this from the start. As we saw earlier, the husband who needs six or eight requests to do something is not unique, and in most cases, not bad-willed, either. He is just a man and that is how men are wired. We're just a bit thick.

But, if a woman starts to get harsh and demanding, men tend to shut down. They don't like to be controlled. The smart woman will ask her husband the eighth time just as sweetly as she asked the first time. One young wife had a wonderful way of dealing with her husband's lethargy. She said to him, "I hope I'm not nagging, but it would really be nice if you would clear out the garage a bit so I could pull my car in."

The wife of Mark Gungor, who created the series "Laugh Your Way to A Better Marriage," would sit down

---

[13] Andelin, *Fascinating Womanhood*, 121–22.

next to him on the couch, and urge him, "Oh please clean out the garage. Ple-e-e-ese." Then she would gently pinch his cheeks and say "Ple-e-e-ese," again. He did it.

Here is his advice to wives to get their husbands to do something:

1. Ask more than once. We already covered that.

2. Ask the right way. Don't be mean. Women may respond to meanness, but men don't. They shut down.

3. Provide positive reinforcement. Always, always thank your husband for *every* little thing that he does. Always! Men love praise and will do more and more for their wife, in proportion to the praise they receive.

4. Barter with him. Figure out what he likes and say, "Would you like _____?" "Yeah," he responds. "Well, if you do this for me, I will do _____." It will usually get done. Is this manipulation? Hardly. Is it manipulation when you agree to work for someone and get paid so much a week? As Gungor says, "Men like to barter."[14]

And, as we mentioned earlier, writing a "honey-do" list on a dry-erase board is a good way to keep the topic alive without nagging. Adding a heart or priority number next to some items can make known the importance of the job. (Come to think of it, we mentioned much of this in Chapter III, but it is so important that it bears repeating.)

---

[14] Mark Gungor, *Laughing Your Way to A Better Marriage* (New York: Simon & Schuster, 2008), 100–8.

HURRIED WOMAN SYNDROME

Sometimes women are so good at getting things done, they become work-aholics or do-aholics. They clean the house, drive the kids to soccer practices and games, do the laundry, feed the dog, bring the car in for service, and they wonder why they have no time for their husband. Actually, for her to have time for and patience with her husband, she needs to take some time for herself.

I was amazed to hear one mother tell me, "I feel guilty that I play tennis twice a week."

I asked her, "Do you fulfill your duties at home?"

"Yes," she answered.

"Then playing tennis twice a week probably makes you a better wife and mother. Do it for them," I offered.

She was delighted with that advice.

A wife needs to have some fun and she needs to do something useful several times a week, if not daily. Marriage writer Laura Doyle says her fun activities include "going to a bookstore, watching my favorite TV show, and having lunch with a friend." For useful activities, she includes going to the gym and washing the windows.[15] Your activities may not be the same for each category, but you get the idea.

Kathryn Sansone, a lovely young mother of ten, preaches the same thing in her book, *Woman First, Family Always*. She writes that after a few years of marriage, "I began to understand that unless I took care of myself, everything in life would seem too difficult, too unmanageable, and definitely not enjoyable.... Was I ready to take care of myself, or would I let myself get pulled down the road where a negative, powerless

---

[15] Doyle, *The Surrendered Wife*, 73.

attitude toward life holds sway? I chose the former and it has made all the difference."[16]

Here's what Kathryn suggests. Take a nice warm bath to relax before bed. She lights some candles for the occasion. She suggests taking a walk in a nature reserve; or driving out into the country; or taking a nap; or getting a massage; or going to the gym. Sometimes she "hibernates," i.e., she cancels all but the barebones necessities, she skips the gym and just rests for one, two, or more days. Of course, an essential part of her program is to learn to say no to people. And she gets help from others when she needs it. As a devout Catholic, she makes time for prayer alone—in various settings, including in a nearby chapel—or with her family. This woman has ten children and she is not burning herself out![17]

Is it selfish for women to take time for themselves? No. It's a virtue to get the sleep you need, the recreation you enjoy, etc. It is part of the virtue of humility: "I know I have some needs and that I am not superwoman."

PLAYFUL ANGER[18]

Is there a way for a woman to get angry at her man without harshness and without setting her heart against him? Is there a way of getting angry that will amuse him rather than anger him? A way that shows her to be above nastiness and bitterness? Absolutely. It's what I would call "playful anger."

Basically, here's how it works: The woman becomes "adorably angry." She threatens never to speak to him

---

[16] Kathryn Sansone, *Woman First, Family Always* (Des Moines: Meredith Books, 2006), 19.

[17] Ibid., 31–33; 37–39; 48–49; 54.

[18] Not everyone may like this section!

again, and as she walks away, she looks back to see
if he is taking her seriously. This exaggeration makes
the man want to laugh. It makes him feel stronger,
sensible, like a real man. This sauciness, says Andelin,
is most attractive to a man, and is far better than the
nastiness of a woman at war, or resentful silence.[19]

Andelin's guidelines for playful anger include:

> 1. Eliminate all bitterness, resentment, sarcasm,
> hate, and ugliness.

> 2. Use only adjectives which will uphold his
> masculinity, such as big, tough, lug, brute,
> hardheaded, stiff-necked, or hairy beast.
> Never use imp, nerd, wimp, little, creep, or
> jerk. Whether he's four-eleven or six-five, he's
> always "big."

> 3. Exaggerate. For example, "What's a big brute
> like you doing picking on a poor, defenseless
> woman like me?" Or make an exaggerated
> threat such as "I'll never speak to you again!"[20]

One woman Andelin describes had had a miserable
marriage for eight years. She started being more positive and loving as taught in *Fascinating Womanhood*,
and things improved. One day her husband was telling
a young marriage-minded bachelor he should think
twice before marrying. "Look at all the headaches a
wife can bring." He kept going on and on, knowing
she was very much within earshot.

Finally, she had had enough. She decided to try
playful anger. She turned to him, stomped her foot,
and said, "You big hairy beast! I'm never going to like
you again, ever!" As she left the room she looked back

---

[19] Andelin, *Fascinating Womanhood*, 320–21.
[20] Ibid., 322–23.

with a faint smile. Her husband was grinning from ear to ear as he said to the young man, "Did you hear what she called me?"

When she got to her bedroom she wondered, "Great, but what now?" He had never once apologized in eight years. But just minutes later he came in and said "I'm sorry and I didn't mean to hurt your feelings. Will you forgive me?" She writes, "I'd have forgiven him anything at that moment."

Two months later he gave her a birthday card—his first ever. It had a cute little hairy beast on the front, and on the inside he had written, "Happy Birthday, Lovingly, your Hairy Beast."[21]

---

[21] Ibid., 329. There is new version of *Fascinating Womanhood*, updated to reflect some of the cultural changes that have occurred since the book was first published, updated by Helen Andelin's daughter Dixie Andelin Forsyth at the request of her mother. The title of the newer edition is *Fascinating Womanhood*: Vintage Edition. Alas, although the principles of playful anger are carried over, this story is not to be found in the newer edition.

CHAPTER VII

The Four Temperaments in Marriage

HEN FLORENCE LITTAUER GOT married and went on her honeymoon, she sat one day merrily eating some grapes. Her husband noticed this and asked her, "Do you like grapes?"

"Oh, I love grapes!"

He then said, "Then I assume you'd like to know how to eat them correctly." (Is this guy for real?)

She asked, "What did I do wrong?"

"It's not that you're doing it *wrong*. It's just that you're not doing it *right*," he answered.

Ever the diplomat, she asked, "What am I not doing right?"

"Anyone knows that to eat grapes properly, you cut off a little bunch at a time like this," he said, as he pulled out his nail clipper (ugh!) and cut a branch and gave it to her.

Florence then asked what I would have asked, namely, "Does this make them taste better?"

"It's not for taste. It's so the large bunch will keep its looks longer. The way **you** eat them—just grabbing grapes here and there—leaves the bunch a wreck. Look at what you've done to it! See all those tiny bare stems sticking up all over the place? They ruin the shape of the whole bunch."

Again, Florence took the words right out of my mouth, "Who cares?"

His response was again off the charts, "*I* care, and that should be enough."

Well, Florence, you're married now. Sorry.

But she tried to do something about it, and he did, too. He tried to get her to be more like himself, everything neat and orderly, even the grapes. She tried to get him to be more like herself, happy and unconcerned with details. They were both quite unsuccessful.

Then Florence discovered a book on the four temperaments and came to realize that she and her husband were different personality types, and that neither was necessarily wrong. Well, at least not totally wrong. She was sanguine, and he was melancholic. They both had a good dose of choleric as well. They began to learn to accept each other's personality and adapt accordingly.[1]

Over 400 years BC, the doctor and philosopher Hippocrates proposed that there were four fundamental personality types, or temperaments. He mistakenly presumed that these four types were the result of different liquids predominating in the human body. The four he identified were:

1. Sanguine (blood), which means cheerful. Sanguine people are usually very friendly, lively, and popular.
2. Choleric (chŏ'-ler-ic, from choler, meaning yellow bile), which means irascible. This temperament applies to the achiever, one who is goal-oriented but may offend people by focusing too much on the goal and not on the persons involved.

---

[1] Florence Littauer, *Personality Plus* (Grand Rapids: Revell, 1992), 4–6.

3. Melancholic (black bile), which means excessively gloomy. The melancholy person is often bright, and neat, but tends to focus on the flaws in things, the negative side.
4. Phlegmatic (phlegm), which means sluggish or unexcitable. The phlegmatic person tends to be slow-moving, calm, and even timid.

It seems that virtually no one is strictly one personality type, but most are a combination of two or more types. For example, a person could be 40 percent choleric and 60 percent sanguine, as I am.

Now, although it is helpful for understanding people to identify their natural temperament, it is even more helpful for each of us, as Christians, to realize what we can do, under the influence of grace, to perfect our own temperaments so as to be better persons and better spouses. St. John Chrysostom writes, "Do not talk to me about those who by nature are kindly and modest, for that is not virtue. Tell me rather of the man who can withstand the great violence of his passions and still lead a regulated life."[2] In other words, we don't get much credit for living out our natural virtues, but for overcoming our wrong inclinations to develop our more difficult virtues. So, our question should be, what can we do to take the temperament we have and allow God to use the good points, and help us overcome the bad?

SANGUINES

What can sanguines do? First, try to summarize, rather than give every detail. Avoid exaggerating, and try to listen to what others have to say. Rather than

---

[2] William A. Jurgens, *Faith of the Early Fathers: Volume II* (Collegeville, MN: Liturgical Press, 1979), 107.

always entertaining others (which they may enjoy at times—so don't stop entirely), try to draw them out and get them to speak. Write down the things you need to know (everyone can benefit from that!). Try to keep up with friends. Some of my own sanguine friends will often disappear for several months—or even years—at a time. When they return, they act as if it was just yesterday that we talked. Don't just relate to others, care for them. And, of course, try for some discipline, and organization.[3]

Use your ability to attract people to draw them closer to God. Don't be afraid to bubble over about what God has done for you. St. John Bosco was clearly a sanguine type (as well as an achiever) and he used his wonderful gift to draw thousands of young street boys to God. He brought some of them to sainthood! But John was very organized and cared for his boys personally, and consistently. I often urge sanguine personalities to use their gifts for spreading the faith.

ACHIEVERS (CHOLERICS)

I work with a good number of achievers, and one thing I always have to tell them is to slow down and learn to relax. Most of them schedule too many things, and as a result, rarely get everything they planned done. It's a pride thing, as the achiever thinks, "I can do it all." In the priesthood we call it the Messiah Complex. The truth is, we can't do everything. We have to pick the most important things and just do those things well. Achievers must learn to say no, graciously and in a matter-of-fact way. "Oh, I'm sorry. There is no way I could do that."

---

[3] Ibid., 77–90.

As an "achiever" priest, I don't agree to attend every possible event, but try to attend a few events and spend a good deal of time at each one. In doing so, I feel much more connected to the people. Granted, it's a smaller number of people, but superficial connections with lots of people are not worth much in the Church—or in families.

I used to vacation with some buddies who wanted to do something every minute. Too much. I was later blessed to find some other friends, families, who know how to relax. Now I vacation with them every summer, where the motto for the week is "Time is of no essence." The adults have family hour every night at six o'clock, sitting around in beach chairs, sharing hors d'oeuvres and sodas or beers, while the kids swim or mill around their parents and other relatives or play on the beach. We stay on the beach till eight, at which point some of the mothers comment, "Perhaps we should think about making some dinner." We just relax, and the (well-behaved) kids seem to love it. This is a classic group of vacationers.

Another thing achievers should do is listen to others, and read what others give you. I would not have written this chapter if I had not agreed to read *Personality Plus* when my sanguine friend recommended it. I often write down book titles when people recommend them, even though my first reaction is, "Well, I've read just about everything on this already," because 70 percent of the time the books they recommend are wonderful.

Achievers should also consider the ideas of others when doing a job, and if you use their idea, give them credit, especially if it's your wife or husband. People will love you for recognizing them, and you won't lose a bit of esteem with others. You will also curb your pride, which is always good for the achiever.

The achiever has to work on learning to trust, when things are beyond his power. I meditate on a card with twenty or thirty Scripture passages on trust daily (you can download a copy at my website, www.cfalive.com). Trust is something we can learn, with God's grace.

Achievers, you should try to motivate, not manipulate. Give people room to freely choose what they really should do! And pray for patience.

MELANCHOLICS

How can a melancholic become the person Christ intended him to be? First, he should continue to do things well, with attention to detail, but he should carefully avoid obsessing over trivia. Another charming name for this is being "anal retentive." If he is in a leadership position, he should avoid micro-managing his subordinates. The transformed melancholy leader should choose good people, and after giving them guidance, let them do their job.

One of the most important things a melancholic person can do is to become more positive and upbeat. Stop always focusing on the negative, and try to speak more of the positives in life. A melancholic should take inventory from time to time and count the number of his negative statements or criticisms, and the number of his positive statements or words of praise in a week. There should be two praises for every criticism (especially in marriage).

Florence Littauer gives talks on the four temperaments and then sends each type off in a group to discuss things. When the melancholics discover they are not the only melancholics, they are pleasantly surprised, and then they sometimes see themselves for the first time in the view of others. One man discovered why he had such a terrible marriage, with his superior attitude and lack of humor. He went home and apologized to his wife, and she wept tears of joy that he saw himself for the first time. He gave her a warm (sanguine) hug.[4]

St. Thérèse of Lisieux was melancholy as a child, crying over just about everything, and then crying over the fact that she cried. But when she had her conversion, she became the most cheerful person imaginable. She was a wonderful mimic and often had her Carmelite sisters laughing in tears with her imitations. The sisters were saddened when she missed recreation because she was so much fun.

Everyone loved to be with her since she was so joyful. That's what grace and her strong will to overcome moods did for her! There is no such thing as a joyless saint. St. Teresa of Ávila said, "Lord, deliver us from gloomy saints!"

PHLEGMATICS

What can the phlegmatic person do to become all God meant him to be? The first thing is to try to get motivated. One way to do this is to do the work at hand as a penance, to save souls. St. Thérèse said you could save a soul by picking up a pin. How many more could be saved by doing a dreaded job that needs to be done! Our Lady of Fatima told the children that many souls are lost because they have no one to make sacrifices for them. And reading the lives of the saints would be most important for a phlegmatic, since they provide us with great motivation.

---

[4] Ibid., 91–92.

St. Margaret Mary seems to have been phlegmatic, since she was reticent to do what Jesus told her. Once when she dragged her feet in obeying him, he gave her a much harder task which cost her untold embarrassment. When she became holier, she became quite willing to do God's will. She carried out his will with vigor, especially in promoting the devotion to the Sacred Heart of Jesus. Phlegmatics should pray for such prodding from God (most likely mediated via the world).

Every phlegmatic, in fact every spouse, needs to work at diplomatically expressing dissatisfaction with his or her spouse. Sometimes a phlegmatic spouse will take the "path of least resistance" and complain about nothing, until she can't take it anymore, and then she leaves. No discussion, no counseling, no nothing. Gone. If she had communicated her dissatisfaction, she might have saved the marriage.

How to do that diplomatically? How about, "I need something from you and it's very important . . ." for example. Or, "You have so many good points. There is one thing I would love you to add to those good points . . ."

Phlegmatics also must learn to be decisive. For that, they need the virtue of prudence, making use of past experiences and thinking of what consequences a decision is likely to have in the future. As was the case with the choleric, they must say no when necessary, with firmness. St. Thérèse used to say no so graciously that the person wasn't sure she had said no.

* * *

No matter what personality type we have, the Lord can work with us to cleanse them of their negative aspects . . . if we let him.

CHAPTER VIII

Marriage and Money

M ANY COUPLES FIND THAT THOUGH they had all the money they wanted or needed when single, that's not the case when married. It is so important to be careful about spending your money once you are married. One reason to live simply enough that you are not wasting your money on credit card debt and useless purchases: the Holy Family lived very simply (their son was born in a stable!). Living simply sends a message to the world that there is something more to come after this life, so we need not pursue riches here. (More on simplicity later.)

TITHING

The first consideration for marital finances should be to try to give 10 percent of your income to the Lord. Here is the story of a young couple who began tithing at the very point when their finances were very tight.

> I can still remember the day my husband & I decided to start tithing. We were living in a very small basement apartment of a friend's house. We moved there because our previous landlord was raising our rent every year by the hundreds and we knew that the money would be better spent on a mortgage.
>
> We had wanted a house close to our parish because it had been our parish for several years, but it was proving impossible. The market at the time was fast. Homes were being listed and sold within a week and our price range

didn't help. We had been house hunting for eight months and the only homes we could afford were foreclosed, dilapidated houses. We came back from seeing one of them and I was in tears. That's when my husband said something radical, "Honey, I think we need to start tithing." Needless to say I wasn't very charitable—what an insane idea! We lived on a single income, had bills, had debt, and now we were going to give what little we had and more to God?! God knew our financial problems & obligations and He certainly didn't need our 10 percent! "You're right, He doesn't, but we need His grace and maybe this will help," my husband said. I thought about it, prayed about it, and after a few days of more frustrating house hunting we surrendered to God and started tithing.

Three months passed and with it came bills, car repairs and more dilapidated homes to see. Still, the first check we wrote when we did our monthly budget was to God, and there was always enough money to put food on the table and pay for the essentials. Then one morning, I got an email for a listing of a four-bedroom, three-bath home in our price range. I called my agent and we went to see it that morning. My mouth dropped because I couldn't believe how everything about this home was what I always wanted, *and* it was listed at a low price! Best of all, it was only five minutes from our parish! We immediately signed the contract and started praying. Bidding wars were typical and we found out that afternoon that three other contracts were offered to the owners.

The next day our realtor called and told us they had accepted our contract! That was one of the many miracles of our home. Because

the realtor was not from the area, she under-
priced the house by $30,000. The other con-
tracts offered more money, but the owners
accepted ours because we were the first ones
to see it. And to make sure we knew that this
was a sign from God, the day our contract was
accepted was on the feast day of the patron
saint of our parish.

Eight years have passed since we've started
tithing and God never is outdone in generosity. My husband's job brought him several
promotions and now he is a Unit Chief in
the government. Our children are blessed to
go to amazing Catholic schools because of
the generosity of grants from their schools.
Not only do we have food on the table and a
roof over our heads, God provides more than
enough for us and is more generous to us than
we were to ourselves eight years ago.

Yes, the temptations come, but looking back
at where we were and where God has taken
us, there is no doubt in our hearts & minds
that the first check we write will be to Him.
Another miracle that tithing has given our
family is freedom. Realizing that all belongs
to God and we are stewards means that doing
His will gives us a great sense of peace.

We understand now that God cannot give
you grace unless you open the door for Him
to come into your life. Tithing is about trust—
trusting that God can never be outdone in
generosity, trusting that He will take care of
you & your needs, but most of all trusting in
His will and that His will is Love.[1]

Scripture sings the praises of giving alms. "Prayer
with fasting is good, but better than both is almsgiving

---

[1] Quote from my parishioners, J and M.

with righteousness.... It is better to give alms than to lay up gold. For almsgiving saves from death and purges away every sin. Those who give alms will enjoy a full life..." (Tb 12:8–9).

Does the Bible recommend tithing? It does: "All tithes from the land, whether the seed from the ground or the fruit from the tree, belong to the Lord; they are holy to the Lord" (Lv 27:30). And,

> Will anyone rob God? Yet you are robbing me! But you say, "How are we robbing you?" In your tithes and offerings! You are cursed with a curse, for you are robbing me—the whole nation of you! Bring the full tithe into the storehouse, so that there may be food in my house, and thus put me to the test, says the Lord of hosts; see if I will not open the windows of heaven for you and pour down for you an overflowing blessing. I will rebuke the locust for you, so that it will not destroy the produce of your soil; and your vine in the field shall not be barren, says the Lord of hosts. Then all nations will count you happy, for you will be a land of delight, says the Lord of hosts. (Mal 3:8–12)

I began tithing right out of college. It worked. I have never been short of money. In fact, I don't know anyone who has committed to tithing and has had financial difficulties. No one has ever said to me, "I tithed and ended up in the poorhouse."

Of course, we must concede that not everyone can give 10 percent back to the Lord right away. I encouraged one lawyer friend to start with 2 or 4 percent per year, and try to increase it by 2 percent each year. He did, and now he is quite comfortable giving 10 percent per year.

One young couple was trying to decide whether to give ten percent of their net income or their gross income. So they asked their priest. He must have been Irish because he answered their question with a question, "Do you want your blessings net or gross?" They gave ten percent of their gross.

CREDIT AND CARE

A good rule to follow is to try to never buy anything on credit besides your house and your first car (which should be a car known for low repairs). Once you pay off your first car you should keep making the payments—to yourself, saving for your next car.

Speaking of cars, it is extremely important to take good care of your car. This means having the oil changed on time. (I use synthetic oil because it improves gas mileage and will give you many more miles between changes.)

It is *very* important take care of rust spots, or even places where the paint has chipped off. As soon as you see this on the body of the car, get out some fine sandpaper, sand it off and spray paint it. You can get a can of spray paint (or brush-on paint) online to match your color. The paint color should be listed on the inside of the car door. I am not suggesting this for cosmetic purposes, but to protect your car from rust. Once a spot starts rusting it will grow and get worse and worse until you have a big hole in your car, and the problem is suddenly not so superficial.

The other thing you should take care of is your house. Key items to attend to include the roof, the heating system, and the air conditioning system. Also, get checked yearly for termites. It would be smart to buy a book on how to take care of your house.

HAZARDS & BENEFITS OF CREDIT CARDS

The first key to living Christian simplicity in marriage is to avoid credit card debt. The interest on credit card debt is over 15 percent. So if you carry a balance on your credit card you will be paying a whole lot of interest every month. It's called the credit card treadmill.

Does that mean you should not have a credit card? No, you can actually save money by having a credit card as long as you pay off the full balance every month. A number of credit cards will give you a cash dividend for every dollar you spend, anywhere from 1 to 2 percent. So, if you spend $30,000, you can receive cash back or a dividend of $300–$600. Not bad, huh? And make sure you get a credit card with no annual fee.

How do you make sure you pay your full balance when it is due? Simply arrange for the money to be taken out of your checking account automatically each month.

Of course, you have to be sure that you have money in your account to cover the payment. So, if you don't have much cushion in your checking account (which you will have if you follow this strategy), you need to keep a little piece of paper or a notebook to keep track of your expenses.

Every spouse should have a budget. One husband told me he was concerned at times about the way his wife spent money. I told him that each should have a budget and should stay within that each month. If his wife wants to use up her budget on Hostess Twinkies (I hope she wouldn't!) let her do it. She has to use her discretion and he has to honor her freedom, and vice versa.

PRAYER AND TIME

One young mother urged spouses to pray before going out shopping. Pray to be guided to good prices and to shop wisely. She said it is better to pray *before* shopping rather than praying *after* that your husband won't be upset about your purchases.

She also pointed out that we must strike a balance between saving money and saving time. Our time is worth something, so it doesn't pay to spend an hour just to save a few dollars. She encourages planning meals ahead of time so you don't have to go to the grocery store two or three times a week for ingredients.

Many of the family money-saving bloggers suggest making up your menus for a couple of weeks at a time and then buying groceries each week to fulfill your menu, with no deviations. One mother cautions against bringing children with you to the grocery store lest they request all sorts of extras.

You should clip coupons and watch for ads for specialty items in newspapers and flyers. (One young mother saved $40 per grocery shopping expedition doing this.) Always buy things such as napkins, toilet paper, and paper towels in bulk. Shopping at wholesale stores such as Costco and BJ's can save lots of money.

SHOP AROUND

Shop around for good prices on cell phone service. Just go online and type in "lowest price cell phone service" or "lowest price cell phone family plans" and some good options will pop up. There are many prepaid or automatically-paid programs for greatly reduced fees.

When buying a computer printer, I recommend a Canon inkjet because if you get a printer with five ink cartridges (a must), you can buy generic replacement cartridges for as little as one dollar each. Do they work? Perfectly, and I have been using these for years. Do they void the warranty? Absolutely not. That question was settled in court years ago.

Shop for cartridges on the internet by entering the make and model of the printer and "generic ink cartridges" on a web browser. The best prices are found when you buy twenty cartridges at a time. I have saved hundreds of dollars on cartridges over the years. In fact, about twenty years ago I gave away a printer which took two cartridges (one black and one color) at forty dollars apiece. It was much less expensive to start over with a new printer with less expensive cartridges.

Be sure to comparison shop on the internet. You would be amazed at the variation of prices from one site to another. We once needed a new bulb for a projector. One person saw it for $250 and we decided that this was too much. I went on the internet and found the same item for $110.

There is a fairly new retailer on the internet with amazing prices: Temu. People were a bit nervous at first to see if it would be reliable. I have found them to be quite reliable to date. When I received a wrong product, they quickly sent me a prepaid return label. You can often get better prices on goods by searching a product on eBay. Always seek free shipping, of course. Walmart's online prices are quite competitive as well. (As with Temu, there is a minimum order for free shipping.)

If you want lots of Christian movies, Pure Flix might be the best alternative streaming service, at a competitive annual fee. I don't watch enough movies to buy a subscription so I stream movies from Christiancinema. com for just three or four dollars at a time. You would be surprised at the number of movies on saints you can stream free on YouTube.

If you are looking for good clothing the higher-end consignment shops might be a good place to start. When I was an engineer I would go with my family to a huge high-class but low-priced tag sale each year. I found three or four Brooks Brothers suits that fit for $10 each. They lasted for years!

One smart shopper recommended avoiding "dry clean only" clothes. She also recommended inviting couples over for dinner rather than going out and paying a babysitter.

Home heating oil prices can be competitively negotiated, and some companies will even give you the service contract for free to win your business. Always try to negotiate prices even for mammograms, home security systems (customer referrals), surgeons, etc. When buying a car, check with your insurance agent as certain cars cost more to insure than others. And insurance companies raise their prices yearly, so if you change to a different company from time to time you can often save a good deal of money.

Also, when buying a car, try to negotiate the price—the dealer prep fee can often be refused since the manufacturer pays the dealer for this preparation work. If you are about to buy a car it would be a good move to subscribe to Consumer Reports online to check out the ins and outs of buying a car.

When buying a house, if the realtor asks your yearly income, you may tell him what you make so they have an idea of the maximum priced house you can afford. *But* don't let them tell you what priced house you should buy. They will generally suggest the maximum you can spend on a house for your income. You should decide what you will spend on a house, and it should be quite a bit lower than the maximum for your income. So, just say, "I make $____ per year but the maximum I want to pay for this house is $____."

It is very smart to set up a college fund for your children. The money gets invested and you don't pay any taxes on the profit from the investment as long as the money is used for education once your children are of age.

THE IMPORTANCE OF SIMPLE LIVING

Every Christian is called to live simply. Fr. Thomas Dubay writes in his excellent book, *Happy Are You Poor*, "Scripture scholars seem to be of one mind . . . that most New Testament texts that deal with poverty as an ideal are meant to be applied to all who follow Christ."[2]

If we observe the lives of the saints, we can see that much of their credibility came from the fact that they lived so simply. In their very lives they taught detachment from material goods, and the importance of living for the Kingdom. This gives the Gospel a richness that the world can admire. Even the media—yes the media!—could hardly resist little (St) Mother Teresa of Calcutta, a poor sister who cared for the poor.

St. John Paul II pointed out that parents must teach their children about simplicity:

> Children must grow up with a correct attitude
> of freedom with regard to material goods, by
> adopting a simple and austere lifestyle and
> being fully convinced that "man is more pre-
> cious for what he is than for what he has."[3]

---

[2] Thomas Dubay, SM, *Happy are You Poor: The Simple Life and Spiritual Freedom* (San Francisco: Ignatius Press, 2003), 13.

[3] John Paul II, *Familiaris Consortio*, 37.

DANGER OF RICHES

Jesus warns us of the dangers of riches: "Woe to you that are rich, for you have received your consolation" (Lk 6:24); "Amen, I say to you, it will be hard for a rich man to enter the Kingdom of heaven. Again, I tell you, it is easier for a camel to go through the eye of a needle than for a rich man to enter the Kingdom of God" (Mt 19:23–24).

Why is the Lord so hard on the rich? St. Ignatius of Loyola writes in the *Spiritual Exercises*: "[The devil] bids [his demons] first to tempt men with the lust of riches . . . that they may thereby more easily gain the empty honor of the world, and then come to unbounded pride. The first step in his snare is that of riches, the second honor, and the third, pride."[4] Pride is the root of every vice.

Well, "I'm not really rich," some will say. "I live comfortably, but I'm not rich." But if we look at world history, we in the US are some of the richest people who have ever lived. And if we look at the other parts of the world, Africa, India, South and Central America, we could hardly be seen as anything but rich.

St. Paul also tells us there is great danger in riches:

> There is great gain in godliness with contentment; for we brought nothing into the world, and we cannot take anything out . . . if we have food and clothing, with these we shall be content. But those who desire to be rich fall into temptation, into a snare, into many senseless and hurtful desires that plunge men into ruin and destruction. For the love of money is the root of all evils; it is through

---

[4] Ignatius of Loyola, *Spiritual Exercises* (Garden City, NY: Doubleday, 1964), 76.

this craving that some have strayed from the faith...(1 Tm 6:6–10)

James has strong words for the rich as well: "For the sun comes up with its scorching heat and dries up the grass, its flower droops, and the beauty of its appearance vanishes. So will the rich person fade away in the midst of his pursuits" (Jas 1:11).

WHATEVER YOU DO FOR THE LEAST...

There is another reason not to be rich: we are responsible for the poor. We cannot live in relative luxury while the poor do not have enough to eat. We find in the first letter of John, "if anyone has the world's goods and sees his brother in need, yet closes his heart against him, how does God's love abide in him? Little children, let us not love in word or speech but in deed and in truth" (1 Jn 3:17).

St. Ambrose had strong words about helping the poor: "You are not making a gift of your possessions to the poor person. You are handing over to him what is his. For, what has been given in common for the use of all, you have claimed for yourself. The world is given to all, and not only to the rich."[5]

Jesus said:

Then he will say to those at his left hand, "Depart from me, you cursed, into the eternal fire prepared for the devil and his angels; for I was hungry and you gave me no food, I was thirsty and you gave me no drink...naked and you did not clothe me, sick and in prison and you did not visit me." They also will answer, "Lord, when did we see you hungry or thirsty...and did not minister to you?"

---

[5] Quoted by Paul VI in *Populorum Progressio* 23.

MARRIAGE for GOD'S SAKE

122

Then he will answer them, "Amen, I say to you, as you did it not to one of the least of these, you did it not to me." And they will go into eternal punishment... (Mt 25:41–46)

Those are powerful words, even frightening. Pope St. John Paul II said in 1979 at Yankee Stadium, "You must never be content to leave [the poor] the crumbs from your feast. You must take of your substance and not just your abundance to help them. And, you must treat them like guests at your family table."[6] Helping the poor is not an option for the Christian.

The following short bibliography is given in case you want to delve deeper into the Christian use of money.

How To Manage Your Money: An In-Depth Bible Study on Personal Finances by Larry Burkett, Moody Publishers, 2002. Burkett is a big name in the Christian use of money.
The Financial Peace Planner: A Step-by-Step Guide to Restoring Your Family's Financial Health by Dave Ramsey, Penguin Books, 1998 (at one point #1 in Christianity on Amazon).

---

[6] Pope John Paul II, Homily at Yankee Stadium, October 2, 1979.

CHAPTER IX
Christian Sex

SEX BETWEEN A HUSBAND AND WIFE should one of the most fulfilling activities they experience. Alas, it often is not, because the husband has been schooled in a very worldly understanding of sex. As a result, the wife is prone to have more and more "headaches" and less and less sex.

THE GOAL

What is the goal for marital relations? It is the same goal for marriage itself. To manifest love for one's spouse and to become one with the spouse, to build personal intimacy, and of course, to bring forth new persons. I speak of personal intimacy and not just intimacy to distinguish between drawing close to a person in all his/her richness, and sharing an intimate act.

Not surprisingly, making other people's lives better (love) and becoming close to others (intimacy) are the two things that fulfill us in the long run. Loving God and neighbor is the condition for entering the Kingdom of heaven (Lk 10:27). Intimacy often follows love. It could be called the "crown" of love.

INTIMACY

That should be on the mind of both as they engage in the marital act: to pursue intimacy above all, not excluding pleasure. So, time spent talking to each other, embracing each other, resting her head on his breast for a time, etc. . . . All these things cultivate a sense of closeness and enrich the partners a great deal. And, of course, these things set the stage for beautiful sexual intimacy.

So how do husband and wife express love in the marital act? That may seem like a strange question, but in fact, having sex can often *not* be an expression of love but an expression of selfishness.

IRONS AND MATCHES

The husband is often called upon to be a leader in the family and his most important leadership function is to initiate love. But to do this, he needs to understand the physical differences between him and his wife: the fact that women are generally like (electric) irons and men are more like matches. (There are exceptions to this analogy but by and large it holds true.) A woman needs time to warm up to having sex whereas a man seems to be ready in an instant. Equally important is the fact that a woman takes time to cool off after reaching a climax, whereas a man tends to cool off immediately, like the extinguishing of a match.

If a man is not aware of this difference and if he does not try to adapt to the tempo of his wife, sex can be quite unsatisfying for her. In time she can lose interest, since she realizes she is simply being used as an object to satisfy her husband's urges. Where is the love in that?

There is something very important about how a man and wife have marital relations. Vatican II taught about conjugal love as follows:

> This [conjugal] love is uniquely expressed and perfected through the act proper to marriage. Hence, the actions within marriage by which

the couple are united intimately and chastely are noble and worthy. Expressed in a manner which is truly human, these actions signify and foster the mutual self-donation by which spouses enrich each other with a joyful and a ready mind.[1]

By saying the marriage act "expresses" and "perfects" conjugal love, the Council was saying that this act celebrates the existence of this love, proclaims it, and by perfecting it, forms the future of this love. As such, the act should be carried out in a way that is truly loving. A way that is primarily aimed at pleasing the *other*, not the self. In this way it will help the love between husband and wife to grow. This act will not only be a *fruit* of making the lifelong commitment of marriage, but a way of fostering and nourishing that love.

So, from what we have said, a man must accommodate his wife's tempo and take the time to relate to her with words and affection to bring her to the point where she strongly desires sexual intimacy. As an iron takes time to heat up once it is plugged in, so a woman needs time to warm up sexually. A man, then, must be patient in order to show his concern for his wife's natural fulfillment in the marriage act. It usually requires both words and action.

As one bride-to-be put it, "I want to be made love to verbally before we make love physically." In other words, it is a very smart thing, indeed a very loving thing, for a husband to spend some time speaking about intimate things, holding her close for a time, before having relations. The best sex is not the most passionate, but the most personal.

---

[1] *Gaudium et Spes*, n. 49. Translation is mine.

One husband told me he got into the habit of spending ten to fifteen minutes every night talking with his wife about how her day went. How good was their sex life? VERY good.

AFFECTION

As we saw earlier, the sharing of affection is something that in this age seems to have been relegated to a mere prelude to sex. Affection should be a delightful language of love quite apart from sexual intimacy. In fact, I believe an important element of a chaste courtship should be developing ways to share affection without the intention of having sex. These ways should become a habit during courtship so that they will be continued in marriage.

Some marriage writers say that a woman may need several days of loving affection before she is ready to have sexual intimacy with her husband. This includes kind words, praises, gentle touches, and, most especially, warm hugs, long and tender. One man in his sixties lamented that his wife didn't want to have sex with him anymore. I asked him when was the last time he hugged her. "It was three years ago. When I hugged her then, she told me it had been two years since I had hugged her before that." (!)

I told him, "No wonder she doesn't want to have sex. You never show her any affection. I want you to go home and start hugging her several times a day. Start with just one or two daily. Otherwise she might think you are drunk."

On a more serious note, hugs in themselves are an extremely important activity for husband and wife, on a daily basis. They are a wonderful sign of solidarity, and of intimacy. In fact, as we saw above, lengthy hugging (twenty seconds or more) in marriage has a measurable beneficial effect on the partners, including the production of oxytocin (a bonding chemical), reduced blood pressure, and a reduction in cortisol (a stress hormone) in the woman.[2] There is a positive effect on the husband as well.

Having said that, when marital relations are intended, a husband should take plenty of time to prepare his wife with affectionate touches, hugs, and words. When things warm up, he needs to touch her in sensitive areas. This, of course, is not mere affection, but sexual foreplay, to keep her ascending to where she ardently desires to complete the sexual act. (To find the sensitive parts of a woman's body, simply type that into a search engine and up they will come.)

Taking the time to prepare his wife may require some self-control for a man because he has to try not to reach a climax too soon. He may have to move more slowly and even just hold her for a few seconds to contain himself. The goal is to delay his own gratification until she reaches a high point. It is a sign of success for the husband if his wife regularly has an orgasm during sexual intimacy.

Even Catholic moral theology acknowledges this difference in tempo, by allowing the man to stimulate his wife right after he reaches a climax if necessary, to ensure that she might also.[3] Of course, this may

---

[2] "How hugs can aid women's hearts," BBC News, August 8, 2005, http://news.bbc.co.uk/2/hi/health/4131508.stm.

[3] See, for example: Germain Grisez, *The Way of The Lord Jesus*, Volume II: Living A Christian Life (Quincy, IL: Franciscan Press, 1993), 642. Grisez acknowledges that either the husband or the wife may perform this stimulation on herself. See also: John R. Cavanagh, *Fundamental Marriage Counseling* (Milwaukee: Bruce Publishing, 1962), 170. Vice versa is not permitted because there should be no need for it after he reaches a climax.

not be necessary if the man accommodates his wife adequately. This is all part of the love and respect a man vowed to have for his wife.

Once he reaches a climax, he proves his love for his wife by attending to her affectionately as she gently descends from her sexual high, and not simply rolling over and going to sleep. Men who accommodate their wives in this way bring upon themselves untold blessings ... and of course a lot more sex than men who don't do this.

COACH HIM

Now, what if your husband knows nothing about this and does as so many American men do, going into marital intimacy looking for pleasure, pleasure, pleasure, without any knowledge of a woman's tempo or any desire to accommodate her? When it comes to sex, he sees her as a pleasure object. Should she say anything? Of course she should, but she needs to be diplomatic. If she tells him, "You're a loser in bed," it won't go well.

She could simply say, "Do you know how slow women are to get interested in sex and how slow we are to descend from a sexual high?" You can use the iron and match comparison if you like. Then you can show him the paragraphs above and ask him to give it some thought. Don't insist on a commitment right away, since when pushed, men often push back. Give it some time. Will you have to mention it again? Probably, but remember when you want a man to do something you must ask him just as sweetly the eighth time as the first.

Is it worth it? Absolutely. If he reforms, not only will you enjoy sex a whole lot more, but your husband will be a whole lot more considerate and loving. He might even gain more than you will.

Pius XII in an address to midwives in October 1951 showed great insight for married couples regarding respect:

> There are some who would allege that happiness in marriage is in direct proportion to the reciprocal enjoyment in conjugal relations. It is not so: indeed, happiness in marriage is in direct proportion to the mutual respect of the partners, even in their intimate relations; not that they regard as immoral and refuse what nature offers and what the Creator has given, but because this respect, and the mutual esteem which it produces, is one of the strongest elements of a pure love, and for this reason all the more tender.[4]

The overarching principle in sexual intimacy for Christians is to pursue love and accommodation above all. Love must always come first for the disciple of Christ. The second goal should be to manifest signs of intimacy. Thus, hugs and tender caresses should be ubiquitous, not only when sharing marital intimacy, but every day. Daily interactions and sexual relations are connected. Personal, affective intimacy should be a major goal in marriage and in the marriage act (which, alas, is not always terribly intimate). And third, of course, they should rejoice in the immense pleasure God has included in this act. The marriage act should be a celebration of the marriage covenant—loving, personally intimate, and delightful.

Is it possible that one or the other could tend to seek too much intimacy, more than the spouse can

---

[4] Pius XII, "Address to Midwives on the Nature of their Profession," October 29, 1951, AAS XLIII (1951), nn. 835–54. English tr. In Odile M. Liebard, *Love and Sexuality (Official Catholic Teachings)* (Minneapolis, MN: Consortium Press, 1978), 101ff.

handle? Yes, rarely. But that is a much more noble selfishness if you will, than pursuing pleasure above all. Also, intimacy just about demands love for it to be established. And love is the foundation of marriage.

It is the usual case that in marriage a man will be more interested in sex than his wife. (There are of course exceptions to this rule.) But in the majority of cases if the man would like to have a good deal of sex, with a wife who is involved and not passively acquiescing, he needs to pursue lots of love. The man who says sweet things to his wife, and who delights in listening to her and holds her close in bed or elsewhere without always anticipating that sex will follow, will be richly rewarded in every way.

The man who is nice to his wife just so she will want to have sex is falling short of Christian benevolence. As we saw earlier, the *Christian* man loves his wife because he vowed to love her, and love is a requirement for salvation. If his love results in more and better sex, as it probably will, so much the better. But the reward of loving behavior runs far deeper than that.

BEDROOM LIMITATIONS?

Are there moral limits as to what husband and wife can do in terms of sexual intimacy? Yes, indeed. While all dignified types of foreplay are allowed, the encounter must always end in natural intercourse with the penis in the vagina. Although oral-genital contact stimulation is not condemned by all theologians as foreplay if mutually agreed upon, my own opinion is that this should be avoided.[5] Why? In a

---

[5] See Thomas G. Morrow, "Rethinking Marital Foreplay," *Homiletic & Pastoral Review*, May 2010, 58–63. For a more detailed analysis of this subject, see Ronald L. Conte, Jr., "Unnatural sexual acts

nutshell, because this sort of activity is impersonal, and sexual encounters should be personal to maintain human dignity. And, of course, if this activity is repugnant to either party, it would be wrong for the other to seek it. I think it is safe to say that anal-genital contact is not licit, since it is not only impersonal but hazardous to one's health. Also, it hardly seems in keeping with human dignity.

In any case, couples should never allow pleasure to become the main goal of sexual intercourse, as is often the case when one or both seek various sorts of "creative" foreplay. In that same address to midwives quoted earlier, Pope Pius XII warns against becoming slaves of sensuality in marriage when he writes, "the gravity and sanctity of the Christian moral law do not admit an unchecked satisfaction of the sexual instinct tending only to pleasure and enjoyment."[6] However, there is no harm in seeking pleasure in the conjugal act as a secondary goal:

> Husband and wife, therefore, by seeking and enjoying this pleasure do no wrong whatever. They accept what the Creator has destined for them. Nevertheless, here also, husband and wife must know how to keep themselves within the limits of a just moderation. As with the pleasure of food and drink so with the sexual they must not abandon themselves without restraint to the impulses of the senses.[7]

One other thought regarding limits. When a couple does anything that inevitably arouses either one

as marital foreplay," February 20, 2011, http://www.catechism.cc/articles/marital-foreplay.htm.
[6] Pius XII, "Address to Midwives," nn. 835–54.
[7] Ibid.

(usually the man gets aroused first), they should plan on having sex. A couple came to see me once because the husband was very upset. His wife had invited him to join her in the shower one morning (presumably to save water), and when he wanted to have sex, she wasn't interested. He was right to be angry. If a wife doesn't want to have sex, she shouldn't invite her husband to shower with her.

CHAPTER X

Natural Family Planning's Good News

GREG AND JULIE REVISITED

In an earlier chapter I promised to give the rest of the story of Greg and Julie Alexander. It is quite a story.

They began to pray that God would deliver them from their mess, and if he did, they would work in marriage and family ministry in the Church. God answered their prayers. They both quit their jobs and soon after they took jobs as coordinators in their diocesan Family Life Office. Greg felt remorse over his vasectomy, but his priest told him he need not have it reversed.

When they attended a marriage conference in Denver six months later, Greg began to wonder if perhaps God wanted him to have a reversal. The more they prayed, the more God seemed to be opening doors for a reversal. Finally, Greg told Julie he couldn't continue in their ministry to married couples knowing he himself was not living what they were teaching. They prayed about it big time.

They found a book while setting up their office, *Physicians Healed*, in which doctors told their own stories of converting from promoting contraceptives to promoting marital chastity (natural family planning). They discovered one doctor nearby who did reversals and made an appointment to see him. Meanwhile Greg was doing some research on the internet, and the cost for this surgery ranged from $5,000 to $15,000. He prayed to God, "Are you really asking me to do this?"

When they got to Dr. Leverett's office they told him their story, and he shared his own story: from doing vasectomies to doing reversals, after reading the Bible one day. They made the appointment on the spot. "But wait, how will we pay for it?"

The good doctor thought a moment and then said, "I like the ministry you are doing so much I want to invest in it. Come next Tuesday and bring $500." All three wept for joy.

They went for the operation and shortly after they learned it was a success. Seventeen months later they gave birth to their third child, Katharine Alexander. Greg commented, "What a blessing! I cannot even begin to put into words what joy she brought into our lives. And to think that we were once closed to receiving a gift such as her..." Four years later they welcomed their fourth child, Michael Gregory Alexander!

That wasn't the end. They had three more children after Michael. They now have *seven* children! What a grace! Once they began to live God's plan for their marriage, so many things fell into place. They still have their struggles, but they now have a happy marriage and seven children.[1]

A huge issue in marriage can be that of birth control. The Church's position on this is very often misunderstood. The following is my attempt to allay that misunderstanding.[2]

---

[1] For the full faith-filled story on Greg and Julie's transformation, see Greg and Julie Alexander, "We Had Everything... But Happiness," *One More Soul*, December 6, 2009, https://onemoresoul.com/marriage-children/testimonials/we-had-everything-but-happiness.html.
[2] The following four sections are from my article, "Contraception and NFP: The Difference," *The Priest Magazine*, June 2016, 34–37.

SEX IS A UNIQUE ACT

The first consideration regarding the use of birth control is the fact that the conjugal act is not some peripheral, or merely biological act which does not engage the person. It is rather a highly personal act which touches a person at his/her core. One can attempt to relegate it to the periphery of one's experience, but most people understand sexual intimacy as far more than a recreational activity. Of course, one may do violence to the essential meaning of a conjugal act by treating it as merely an act of pleasure without any other significance (as in "hooking up"). But most intelligent, reflective persons would see this as in fact "doing violence" to the very nature of sexual intimacy.

Our laws reflect this. To verbally abuse a child is considered bad enough, but to sexually abuse a child calls for prosecution and incarceration. And well it should. Our laws acknowledge that sexual contact is unique and has a profound effect on the person. Thus, arguments that contraception is analogous to using ear plugs or using sunglasses fail to take into account that the sex act is unique insofar as it has a profound effect on the participants. It is a kind of core act unlike hearing or seeing.

It is more analogous to a kiss, with all the rich meaning of that act. The kiss of Judas is considered deplorable because it made use of a sign of affection and love to turn Jesus over to his enemies. It was a shameful lie.

"ANTI-LIFE" MENTALITY

Contraception is said to brand its participants with an "anti-life mentality" as Pope Saint John Paul II writes in *Familiaris Consortio*:

Scientific and technological progress, which contemporary man is continually expanding in his dominion over nature, not only offers the hope of creating a new and better humanity, but also causes ever greater anxiety regarding the future. Some ask themselves if it is a good thing to be alive or if it would be better never to have been born; they doubt therefore if it is right to bring others into life when perhaps they will curse their existence in a cruel world with unforeseeable terrors. Others consider themselves to be the only ones for whom the advantages of technology are intended and they exclude others by imposing on them contraceptives or even worse means. Still others imprisoned in a consumer mentality and whose sole concern is to bring about a continual growth of material goods, finish by ceasing to understand, and thus by refusing, the spiritual riches of a new human life. The ultimate reason for these mentalities is the absence in people's hearts of God, whose love alone is stronger than all the world's fears and can conquer them.

Thus an *anti-life mentality* is born, as can be seen in many current issues: One thinks, for example, of a certain panic deriving from the studies of ecologists and futurologists on population growth, which sometimes exaggerate the danger of demographic increase to the quality of life.

But the church firmly believes that human life, even if weak and suffering, is always a splendid gift of God's goodness. Against the pessimism and selfishness which cast a shadow over the world, the church stands for life: In each human life she sees the splendor of that "yes," that "amen," who is Christ himself. To the "no" which assails and afflicts the

world, she replies with this living "yes," thus
defending the human person and the world
from all who plot against and harm life.[3]

Of course, when a couple contracepts it is usually
not because they are against life, or do not value life.
However, when they contracept they slide into this
negative view of human life because the act of contraception is an effort to prevent a life from being
conceived, in a deeply personal human act.

It is analogous to what happens to a man who uses
pornography. When a man looks at pornography he
ordinarily doesn't begin to do so because he holds
women in low esteem, or considers them as mere
objects of enjoyment. However, once he has used pornography for a time, that is the mentality he emerges
with. Women are subconsciously seen as playthings,
objects of use.

AN EXCLUDING LOVE

As we saw above, conjugal love symbolizes married
love and forms the future of that love. So, the symbolism of the marriage act has a formative power for
the couple.

Now, the symbolism of contracepted sex is to communicate love toward one's spouse, but at the same
time to exclude children. It is akin to what the French
call an *égoïsme a deux*. When a couple has sex, they not
only symbolize their marital commitment of love, but
they also form their love, in this case, an excluding
sort of love.

It is not the intention to have no more children
that is the problem. That is an acceptable intention
for just reasons. It is the act of contracepted marital

---

[3] *Familiaris Consortio*, n. 31. Emphasis added.

intimacy itself in its rich symbolism which forms a love that excludes others.

NOT TOTAL SELF-GIVING

Pope Saint John Paul II writes:

> When couples, by means of recourse to con-
> traception, separate these two meanings that
> God the creator has inscribed in the being of
> man and woman and in the dynamism of
> their sexual communion, they act as "arbiters"
> of the divine plan and they "manipulate" and
> degrade human sexuality and with it them-
> selves and their married partner by altering its
> value of "total" self-giving. Thus, the innate
> language that expresses the total reciprocal
> self-giving of husband and wife is overlaid,
> through contraception, by an objectively con-
> tradictory language, namely, that of not giving
> oneself totally to the other. This leads not
> only to a positive refusal to be open to life,
> but also to a falsification of the inner truth
> of conjugal love, which is called upon to give
> itself in personal totality.
>
> When, instead, by means of recourse to
> periods of infertility, the couple respect the
> inseparable connection between the unitive
> and procreative meanings of human sexuality,
> they are acting as "ministers" of God's plan
> and they "benefit from" their sexuality accord-
> ing to the original dynamism of "total" self-
> giving, without manipulation or alteration.[4]

In other words, when using contraception the spouses are in essence saying, "I give you all of myself except my fertility," and "I want all of you except your fertility." This falls short of an authentically total self-gift.

---

[4] *Familiaris Consortio*, n. 32.

So, it seems that contraception has a powerful negative spiritual effect on those who use it, not to mention all the medical drawbacks it entails. Natural family planning, on the other hand, is a wonderfully "green" way of controlling family size, one that avoids all the negatives of contraception. It involves a similar intention as in contraception, but an entirely different exercise of a profoundly formative act.

Is this an easily understood difference? No, it is subtle and requires some thought to grasp. But it is true, and understanding this is a key to marital happiness.

NATURAL FAMILY PLANNING BENEFITS

Many people—and many Catholics—have never heard of natural family planning. It has been called the best-kept secret in the Catholic Church.

NFP EFFECTIVENESS

The effectiveness of NFP (if used correctly) is about 99 percent, or even higher. In a 2006 study done by a team at the University of Heidelberg in Germany, in which 900 women were tracked using the symptothermal method (STM), avoiding sex during fertile periods, the failure rate was 0.4 percent.[5]

The World Health Organization performed a study involving 869 fertile women from Australia, India, Ireland, the Philippines, and El Salvador. They found that 93 percent were able to correctly interpret their body's fertility signs regardless of education levels or culture.[6]

---

[5] European Society for Human Reproduction and Embryology, "Natural Family Planning Method As Effective As Contraceptive Pill, New Research Finds," *Science Daily*, February 21, 2007, www.sciencedaily.com/releases/2007/02/070221065200.htm.

[6] R. E. Ryder, "'Natural family planning': effective birth control

Marquette University developed a new method of NFP using the ClearBlue Easy fertility monitor and cycle history to determine fertility.[7] The monitor measures estrogen and luteinizing hormone via urine samples. This method works during the postpartum period, breastfeeding, and perimenopause, and involves shorter abstinence times than other NFP methods.[8] Many couples have been opting for this method because the monitor-reading is precise and is not affected by sleep quality as body temperature can be. It takes just a few minutes a day for the first two weeks (or so) of each menstrual cycle.

Free classes in NFP are available for Catholic couples through https://ccnfp.org/programs/.

Of course, natural family planning requires abstinence during a woman's fertile time, which is also the peak time for libido in both husband and wife. This is because nature is pro-fertility, pro-children.

NFP AND DIVORCE

The divorce rate for church-going NFP users is about half that of those who used contraceptive methods.[9] This is most likely due to the need for more communication by the couple using NFP. Plus, many couples say

---

supported by the Catholic Church," September 18, 1993, https://www.ncbi.nlm.nih.gov/pmc/articles/PMC1678728/.

[7] Mary Schneider, "Institute for Natural Family Planning Model," *Marquette University College of Nursing*, https://www.marquette.edu/nursing/natural-family-planning-model.php.

[8] Richard Fehring and Mary Schneider, "Comparison of Abstinence and Coital Frequency Between 2 Natural Methods of Family Planning," *National Library of Medicine*, 2004, https://pubmed.ncbi.nlm.nih.gov/26227903/.

[9] Richard J. Fehring, "The Influence of Ever Use of Natural Family Planning and Contraceptive Methods on Divorce Rates as Found in the 2006–2010 National Survey of Family Growth," https://www.ncbi.nlm.nih.gov/pmc/articles/PMC4536625/. Informal studies have shown even smaller divorce rates.

the abstinence keeps their love fresh, forcing them to concentrate on the other types of love, namely *agape* (benevolent love), friendship, and affection. One husband stated it was like having a courtship and honeymoon each month.

MORE NFP BENEFITS

NFP uses no pills or external implement to prevent conception. As we mentioned earlier, it's the only "green" method. And it's not expensive. Moreover, it honors a woman's natural cycles of fertility and infertility. This prevents the mindset in the husband that she is always available for marital relations. And husbands are encouraged to get involved by keeping the charts up-to-date.

WITNESS OF NFP USERS

From Jennifer and John Campbell:

> The benefits of NFP extend beyond family planning. We'd heard that often times the husband will develop a deeper respect for his wife and the gift of her fertility. In practice, we've found this to be noticeably true. A constant awareness of cycles and phases makes it easier to perceive when to be loving and gentle, extra patient and thoughtful, and when to resume physical intimacy.[10]

And from a wife,

> My husband is a true gentleman... In our experience with Natural Family Planning, I can tell you that I feel so respected and well cared-for by my husband in a very big way... [He is] my "knight in shining armor."[11]

---

[10] Jennifer and John Campbell, "Connections," https://www.usccb.org/resources/campbell-connections.

[11] Sarah Hammond, "My Husband the Gentleman," 2009, https://www.usccb.org/resources/nfp-my-husband-the-gentleman.pdf.

It has been alleged that wives are more open to using NFP than husbands. Here are some comments by male NFP users:

> Taking our NFP class strengthened my convic-
> tion that the manly thing to do was to protect
> my wife from the harm contraception could
> cause. And, the couples who taught the class
> exuded joy.[12]

> When we try living Church teachings faith-
> fully, we discover how, in actuality, those
> teachings offer us an authentic guide to "the
> good life" [which is also the happy life]; to
> live the way God intended us to live.... How
> do you know the Church teaches "the good
> life"? Perhaps only by experience, after giving
> it a chance...which means to simply commit,
> trust in the wisdom of the Church, and see
> where the fullness of family life takes us. It
> has made me and my wife *very* happy.[13]

THE BLESSING OF CHILDREN

There is something far better than NFP: having children. Sacred Scripture proclaims:

> Certainly sons are a gift from the Lord,
>   the fruit of the womb, a reward....
> Blessed is the man who has filled his quiver
>   with them.
> He will never be shamed... (Ps 27:3, 5)

The Church proclaims similar sentiments:

> By their very nature, the institution of mat-
> rimony itself and conjugal love are ordained

---

[12] Sharon and Mike Phelan, "Escape from Fuddledom," Natural Family Planning Program, 2011, https://www.usccb.org/resources/Phelans-Escape-from-Fuddledom_0.pdf.
[13] Words of A. R., Rockville, MD.

> for the procreation and education of children,
> and find in them their ultimate crown....
>   Children are really the supreme gift of
> marriage and contribute very substantially
> to the welfare of their parents.... Among
> the couples who fulfil their God-given task
> [of procreating] those merit special mention
> who with a gallant heart and with wise and
> common deliberation, undertake to bring up
> suitably even a relatively large family.[14]

Pope St. Paul VI taught,

> In relation to physical, economic, psychologi-
> cal and social conditions, responsible parent-
> hood is exercised, either by the deliberate and
> generous decision to raise a numerous family,
> or by the decision, made for grave motives and
> with due respect for the moral law, to avoid
> [for a time, or] for an indeterminate period,
> a new birth.[15]

Thus, if there are serious physical, economic, psychological or social reasons (a *real* population explosion
would be a possible social reason) not to have a child,
natural family planning can be used to avoid pregnancy.

Can NFP be used to space children? Yes, but the best
way to space children is by breastfeeding. The ideal
spacing for children is said to be about two years. Total
breastfeeding, with no supplements (not even water)
and no pacifiers, makes a woman 98 percent infertile for
the first six months after the birth of a child. In some
cases this infertility continues longer than six months.
Thus, if a mother breastfeeds her child for a little over
a year, the timing of the next child will be ideal.

---

[14] *Gaudium et Spes*, nn. 48, 50.
[15] *Humanae Vitae*, n. 10.

The benefits of breastfeeding for both mother and child far exceed the benefits of child-spacing. And there are groups ready—and indeed, eager—to help women perform this act of love for their children effectively.[16] Thus, if a mother breastfeeds her child for a little over a year, the timing of the next child will be ideal.

CONTRACEPTION: A SERIOUS SIN?

So, what about contraception? Is it a serious sin? A matter of mortal sin? In his 1930 encyclical *Casti Connubii*, Pope Pius XI taught that contraception is a grave matter:

> Any use whatsoever of matrimony exercised in such a way that the act is deliberately frustrated in its natural power to generate life is an offense against the law of God and of nature, and those who indulge in such are branded with the guilt of a grave sin. (n. 56)

In 1975 the Congregation for the Doctrine of the Faith taught in its "Declaration on Sexual Ethics" the following:

> Now, according to Christian tradition and the Church's teaching, and as right reason also recognizes, the moral order of sexuality involves such high values of human life that every direct violation of this order is objectively serious. (n. 10)

---

[16] Dr. William Sears, "Breast Feeding and Fertility," Ask Dr. Sears, 2020, http://www.askdrsears.com/topics/feeding-ting/breastfeeding/faqs/breastfeeding-fertility. Of course, this total form of breastfeeding requires great dedication, but many doctors say the benefits for both mother and child are well worth it. See also Sheila Kippley, *Breastfeeding and Natural Child Spacing* (Cincinnati, OH: Couple to Couple League, 2008).

The footnote attached to this paragraph includes, "Paul VI, encyclical letter '*Humanae Vitae*,' 13, 14" where Pope Paul VI proclaims the immorality of "every action which, either in anticipation of the conjugal act, or in its accomplishment, or in the development of its natural consequences, proposes, whether as an end or as a means, to render procreation impossible."[17]

It should be clear from all this that contraception is a serious sin, and a mortal one if done with knowledge, sufficient reflection, and full consent of the will.

What if a person does not accept the Church's teaching on contraception? Pope John Paul II has an answer for this:

> It is sometimes reported that a large number of Catholics today do not adhere to the teachings of the Church on a number of questions, notably sexual and conjugal morality, divorce and remarriage. Some are reported as not accepting the Church's clear position on abortion. It has also been noted that there is a tendency on the part of some Catholics to be selective in their adherence to the Church's moral teachings. It is sometimes claimed that dissent from the *Magisterium* is totally compatible with being a "good Catholic" and poses no obstacle to the reception of the sacraments. This is a grave error...[18]

Those familiar with Saint John Paul II should be quite aware that his mention of "conjugal morality" would involve the sinfulness of contraception. The

---

[17] See also *Familiaris Consortio*, n. 32.
[18] John Paul II, "Address to the Bishops of the United States in Los Angeles," September 16, 1987, https://www.vatican.va/content/john-paul-ii/en/speeches/1987/september/documents/hf_jp-ii_spe_19870916_vescovi-stati-uniti.html.

defense of *Humanae Vitae* was one of the main hall-marks of his papacy.

The importance of embracing the Church's moral teaching should be clear from the words of Christ to the seventy disciples when he sent them out: "He who hears you hears me, and he who rejects you rejects me, and he who rejects me rejects him who sent me" (Lk 10:16).[19]

CONTRACEPTION'S FURTHER NEGATIVES

We should mention the more serious nature of certain contraceptives in that they are either part-time or full-time abortifacients. For example, the Pill, especially the mini-pill (low estrogen), and the morning-after pill are part-time abortifacients in that they harden the uterus wall to make sure that any breakthrough embryos are flushed out of the woman. The IUD has the same effect.

Barrier methods such as condoms (male or female) and diaphragms with spermicides are rated at 98 percent and 94 percent method effectiveness respectively. (User effectiveness is much lower for condoms.) Vasectomies are quite effective in preventing conception, but there is some evidence that a vasectomy may cause a rare form of dementia in later years.[20]

WHEN ONE SPOUSE INSISTS ON CONTRACEPTION

What if your spouse insists on contraception knowing that you embrace the Church's teaching that it is

---

[19] See also from St. John Henry Cardinal Newman, Hymn "Firmly I Believe and Truly," *Ancient and Modern: Hymns and Songs for Refreshing Worship* (Canterbury Press, 2013), #634a: "And I hold in veneration, for the love of [Christ] alone, Holy Church as his creation, and her teachings as his own."

[20] Marla Paul, "Vasectomy May Put Men at Risk for Type of Dementia," Northwestern Medicine, February 12, 2007, https://news.feinberg.northwestern.edu/2007/02/01/vasectomy/.

seriously sinful? May you have sex with him/her? Yes, under certain conditions.

1. When your own action is not illicit, i.e., you are not the contraceptor.
2. When proportionately grave reasons exist for having sex with your partner (the importance of the sex act for your marital harmony would suffice).
3. As long as you are seeking to help your spouse to cease contracepting (with patience, prayer, charity, and dialogue; though not necessarily at the moment of conjugal intimacy).[21]

The non-contracepting spouse should be highly motivated to help his/her spouse to move to NFP, above all for the salvation of his/her immortal soul. This, of course, should be the main concern for every married person.

The spouse who wants to live the Church's teaching on birth control should strive to be the best and kindest spouse possible to help their spouse be open to natural family planning. This is not the time to try to force the husband/wife to switch to NFP by nagging or unpleasantness. The goal should not be a switch by the spouse to NFP as a reluctant acquiescence. The best transition would be a conversion to the beauty of an integrated Catholic marital life, although a desire to embrace a spouse's moral values out of a deeply respectful love would suffice as a start.

A first step for a reluctant spouse might be to hear some podcasts on the Theology of the Body. This is

---

[21] Pontifical Council for The Family, "Vademecum for Confessors Concerning Some Aspects of the Morality of Conjugal Life," 1997, n. 13.

the profound theology on chastity developed by Pope John Paul II. It has converted thousands of people to embrace biblical and Church teaching on marriage and family.[22]

The next step toward a possible conversion of the spouse would be for the couple to take a class in natural family planning, with follow-up personal interaction with a teaching couple. (This can be done online. For free classes go to https://ccnfp.org/.)

It's not just the learning of NFP technique that is important. More significant is the discovery of the philosophy behind NFP which is most often included in the instruction.

CONVERSION AND CONFESSION

If a person or a couple converts to embrace the Church's teaching on birth control, there is the issue of the Catholic party/parties receiving the sacrament of penance and reconciliation. It seems that a large number of Catholics have never heard the Church's teaching on this subject[23] and so might claim invincible ignorance. So, their choosing contraception would not constitute a mortal sin. Nonetheless, it should be confessed.

If either spouse chose sterilization (pre-conversion), this poses a different sort of issue. In order to be forgiven a spouse would have to sincerely repent of having taken this step. As we saw earlier, reversal would not be required, but there should be genuine regret over having had the procedure in order to worthily receive absolution for it. Again, past invincible

---

[22] I have included a fairly thorough explanation of John Paul II's Theology of the Body in Appendix A of this book.

[23] For the widespread occurrence of this, we priests should take most of the blame.

ignorance could be a mitigating circumstance for the culpability regarding this sin.

And, of course, there should be atonement, beyond the penance given by the priest which is often largely symbolic.

CONCLUSION

So, it seems that contraception has a powerful negative spiritual effect on those who use it, not to mention all the medical drawbacks it entails. Natural family planning, on the other hand, is a wonderfully "green" way of controlling family size, one that avoids all the negatives of contraception. It may involve a similar intention, but is an entirely different exercise of a profoundly formative act.

This is not an easily understood teaching. However, many of those who embrace it report noteworthy blessings in practicing it.

Although NFP is a wonderful blessing for marriage, it is not the best thing. The best thing for marriage is children, conceived in love and raised in the way of the Lord.

CHAPTER XI

Pornography and Marriage

My heart hurts for individuals caught in the web of pornography. When you see grown men crying in your office because they can't quit and when they tell you that porn is costing them everything, you quickly realize that pornography is not just a leisurely activity. Then, when you meet a woman who feels rejected, not good enough, and unloved by her partner because of porn, you want to change something about the way things are being done.[1]
—Kevin B. Skinner, PhD

MATT FRADD TELLS THE STORY OF one particular man in his book, *Delivered*. Mike O'Brien (let's call him) was raised in a good Catholic family. They often prayed together in the evenings, and of course went to Mass every Sunday. In addition, they would participate in prayer meetings on Sunday afternoons. He attended World Youth Day in Denver, a youth conference at Franciscan University in Steubenville, OH, and was captain of his football and baseball teams in high school.

At age twelve he spent a weekend with his friend who introduced him to pornography. Soon thereafter he learned about masturbation and started doing it

---

[1] Kevin B. Skinner, "Is Porn Really Destroying 500,000 Marriages Annually?," *Psychology Today*, December 12, 2011, https://www.psychologytoday.com/us/blog/inside-porn-addiction/201112/is-porn-really-destroying-500000-marriages-annually.

daily. He had learned these things were wrong, but never was told how not to get hooked on them.

When he was a senior a priest taught a class on marriage and chastity and this was the first time he had heard about sex in the context of love and beauty. It really moved him.[2]

MARRIAGE

He met his future wife in college, and when the opportunity presented itself they both took a semester in Rome. Being there in the midst of all the beautiful history of the Church and her martyrs inspired him to turn from pornography, and he fell into it only once while there. When they visited Lourdes he prayed for the virtue of chastity.

Before he married Anne in 2001 he told her about his struggles with pornography. She was happy that he was so honest with her but she feared what this could mean for their marriage.

A week before the wedding he purchased a pornographic magazine thinking it would be his last. He was convinced that when he got married this would no longer be a problem. He was dead wrong. When they got internet, he began to binge on pornography, especially when she was away. When he had sex with Anne all the pornographic images would come to his mind and he couldn't focus on her. There seemed to be a wall between him and his wife. That wall was his obsession with pornography. After a binge he would get to confession and then confess to his wife. This, of course, bothered her a great deal. "Was there something

---

[2] Matt Fradd, *Delivered* (El Cajon, CA: Catholic Answers Press, 2014), 72–74. I strongly recommend this book to anyone struggling with pornography.

wrong with me that he had to look elsewhere?" Her mother and stepfather had divorced due to lust and pornography. Would she divorce over this? She wrote, "Pain consumed me. Anger followed—fueled by fear, loneliness, betrayal, confusion and bitterness."[3] She decided to show her anger by blowing up, yelling, screaming, and calling him names. It didn't work. (Men rarely respond to meanness.)

In time he began to imagine what it would be like to be with other women. He even told his wife he was considering leaving her halfway through their first pregnancy. A week later she had a miscarriage, perhaps due to the cruel words he had spoken. (According to researcher Patrick Fagan, PhD, a psychologist and former Deputy Assistant Health and Human Services Secretary, pornography use is correlated with a 300 percent increase in infidelity.[4])

For three years this nightmare continued. Mike tried to get counseling but no one seemed to be skilled at helping people break free from pornography. A priest suggested some books on the subject, but nothing seemed to help.

ULTIMATUM

Finally, in 2004, Anne gave him an ultimatum: "Get help or we're done." She was surprised when he agreed to get help and try to save the marriage. (One part of her had hoped he would leave and her struggles would end. But she knew she had to do all in her power to save the marriage, to be faithful to God. How right!)

---

[3] Matt Fradd, *Delivered*, 54–55.
[4] Patrick F. Fagan, PhD, "The Effects of Pornography on Individuals, Marriage, Family, and Community," *Marriage and Religion Research Institute*, December 2009, https://downloads.frc.org/EF/EF12D43.pdf.

Mike begged her to give him a chance, and he got very serious about changing. He found a 12-step sexual addiction group through the phone book. (Such groups, like Sexaholics Anonymous, use the same rigorous and effective steps for healing as those used by Alcoholics Anonymous.)

They attended their first Christian counseling session with a man who had himself gone through pornography recovery. Mike felt a hint of hope. The counselor told him he needed to attend a 12-step group every week, call someone in the group daily, read about recovery every day and (most importantly) pray each morning and night.

When he went to his first group meeting, he was pleasantly surprised. The men seemed like regular guys, and very focused on recovery. In his first year and a half he fell back into pornography half a dozen times. He soon found a more intense recovery group and he became much more regular in calling guys and reading recovery materials. Through this group he made some very good friends, Christian men of prayer, who were devoted to their families. He soon was able to go five years without a fall.

ANNE

When they had started counseling, Mike had claimed it was his wife's fault that he had this problem. (It almost never is.) The counselor told him he was flat out wrong. He told them not to watch pornography together, as it cheapens sex and love.

As Mike began to pull out of his addiction, Anne realized she still had some unresolved anger toward him. The counselor had recommended early on that she attend a group for women dealing with an addicted husband. "Why me? He has the problem!" she thought. She was wrong. She still had some terrible behaviors toward him, cursing at him, calling him names, and disrespecting him. She went to a group and found help in her own healing.

Mike was encouraged to compliment his wife daily and pray together with her. It was also suggested that they share their feelings each evening. Anne was slow to warm up to that, but when they did, their intimacy began to blossom.

Mike and Anne attended some talks by Christopher West on Pope John Paul II's Theology of the Body and it helped. But Mike still struggled with the times of abstinence called for in natural family planning. Later he read West's book, *The Good News about Sex and Marriage*, and listened to his recordings on the Theology of the Body, and was converted. He had found a treasure, learning that the marital act was to symbolize the love of Christ and his Church. He delighted in the concept that every time he made love to his wife, he was restating their wedding vows and that their marital union symbolized the Holy Trinity. Ever since, he has never treated Anne as an object of use. The marriage began to thrive.

PERSEVERANCE

After some years Mike became a bit overconfident and attended fewer recovery meetings. He fell several times. He realized his mistake and was confirmed in his journey when he heard a presenter at a Christian sexual addiction talk say he had been clean for over twenty-five years. Yet the presenter still humbly participates in 12-step groups regularly. Mike acknowledges that reading articles by Jason Evert, Matt Fradd, and at ThePornEffect. com have been instrumental in his conversion.

When he read about what happens to the actors in the pornography business, he sobered up dramatically about the attractiveness of what they do. The women are treated like trash off camera. He realized that what he saw as fun before was anything but fun. It was misery.

KEY POINTS

Mike's story illustrates some key points about pornography addiction:[5]

1. **Be completely honest** about your addiction. No denial whatsoever. Some men rationalize that their habit is no problem so they can go on with it. Until they admit their sin, and the harm it does to ALL their relationships, their situation is hopeless. Admitting the truth is step one. When Mike told his wife about his failures, he opened the door to his recovery.

2. **Clean up your environment**. No magazines, no videos; blocking and accountability software such as covenanteyes.com or qustodio.com.[6] One young man kept typing in his password to get to pornography so I invited him to bring in his laptop and have me put in a password. It worked.

3. **Get support and someone to report to weekly**. For addiction, attend a 12-step group such as Sexaholics Anonymous.[7] As Mike did, you need to call a mentor weekly or more to keep yourself in check.

---

[5] Ibid., and Peter Kleponis, PhD, "Pornography Addiction Recovery: Integrity Starts Here," Those Catholic Men, July 12, 2017, https://thosecatholicmen.com/articles/pornography-addiction-recovery-integrity-starts-here/.

[6] There are several other such software packages. Just type "porn blocking software" into a browser and a number of these will show up.

[7] Sexaholics Anonymous has the same criterion for chastity as the Catholic Church: no sexual activity outside marriage.

4. **Get counseling** from someone skilled in this area. A good counselor can help someone identify their triggers, as well as the potential psychological wounds that fostered the desire for pornography.

5. **Pursue a strong spiritual life**. This should be first in importance. For a Catholic, I would recommend a daily rosary (with short meditations for each mystery) with your spouse, frequent if not daily Mass (every Catholic should pray this prayer: Lord, if you would like me to go to Mass daily, please arrange it), frequent confession, spiritual direction, retreats, Scripture study, weekly fasting, and Catholic men's groups such as "That Man Is You" and the Knights of Columbus.

6. **Read books** on pornography addiction recovery.

7. **Pursue all the virtues**, not just temperance. Start with the four cardinal virtues: prudence, justice, temperance, and fortitude. Read about these and the parts of each.

If you follow this program with zeal you might not only kick the pornography habit; you might just become a saint, which is the best thing you could ever do.

Another point we can glean from Mike's story is that men sometimes think that when they get married their pornography compulsion will fade away. The thought is that once a man has sexual relations with his wife, he will not need pornography. The problem is, the sex of pornography and that in marriage are two vastly different things. The sex of pornography is a selfish pursuit of pleasure in an impersonal act which sees a woman as an object of use. The sex of marriage, on the other hand, is a beautiful manifestation of intimacy with a treasured person, for whom the man wants to sacrifice himself as Christ sacrificed himself for the Church. The desire for pornography doesn't go away when a man marries.

Sex in marriage is a sad caricature if it is merely for self-gratification. Personal intimacy is what fulfills both husbands and wives in the long run, not pleasure.

Of course, another point, made by Mike's counselors, is that couples should never watch pornography together. Some antiquated psychologists still recommend this as a way to wean men off pornography. It doesn't work. It just cheapens the bedroom.

Another point from the story of Mike and Anne: a wife often needs counseling too. It may not seem fair, but she will have some healing to do after helping him out of his "cruel slavery to lust."

One more point: it's not her fault. A man who blames his wife for his addiction is in a dream world, a nightmare world. As long as he clings to that lie he will never recover.

WOMEN

It is not just men who struggle with pornography addiction. Thirty percent of pornography users are women. Some women get hooked on pornography from an early age and can't stop. There are several web sites that offer help to addicted women.[8]

What is it like for the women in pornographic movies? Here is the witness of one performer. After her husband took some pictures of her and sent them out, she went to Los Angeles to meet with an agent.

---

[8] One of them is http://www.covenanteyes.com/2014/06/30/resources-women-struggle-porn/.

I met with the agent in his filthy apartment. He told me I could make a lot of money in this business but first I had to show him how "good" I was.... I wadded up whatever self-worth I had in me and threw it out the window. He set up his cheesy video equipment and I did my first "scene" right there in his crappy apartment, with no condom and no protection. It was humiliating and disgusting. After he was done violating me, he made up a bogus contract and sent me home. I never got any work from him.[9]

Speaking of other pornography sessions, she related,

I tried to convince myself that I would get used to making porn, or that things would get better. They never did.... The sheer guilt, along with the emotional and physical exhaustion drove me even deeper into depression. I didn't even know who I was anymore.[10]

She later made her way out of this gruesome way of living with the help of the Lord Jesus.

Dr. Mary Ann Layden reported,

Once [the pornography actresses] are in the industry they have high rates of substance abuse, typically alcohol and cocaine, depression, borderline personality disorder.... The experience I find most common among the performers is that they have to be drunk, high or dissociated in order to go to work. Their work environment is particularly toxic.... The terrible work life of the pornography performer is often followed by an equally terrible home life. They have an increased risk of sexually transmitted disease (including HIV),

---

[9] Fradd, *Delivered*, 64. Story by April Garris.
[10] Ibid., 65.

domestic violence and have about a 25 percent chance of making a marriage that lasts as long as 3 years.[11]

66 percent of pornography performers have herpes; 12 to 28 percent have another STD; and 7 percent are HIV positive.[12]

Any person who could use pornography after knowing what the performers go through would have to have a heart of stone.

PREVALENCE OF PORNOGRAPHY USE

The story of Mike and Anne is a dramatic one, but how widespread is the use of pornography in this age? Very. Forty million Americans regularly visit porn sites. About 200,000 Americans are "porn addicts." Thirty-five percent of all internet downloads are related to pornography. Twenty-five percent of all search engine queries are related to pornography, or about 68 million search queries a day. The American Academy of Matrimonial Lawyers found in a 2002 survey of their lawyers that "an obsessive interest in internet pornography" was a significant factor in 56 percent of their divorce cases the prior year.[13]

---

[11] Judith Reisman, Jeffrey Sanitover, Mary Anne Layden, and James B. Weaver, "Hearing on the brain science behind pornography addiction and the effects of addiction on families and communities," Hearing to U. S. Senate Committee on Commerce, Science & Transportation, November 18, 2004, accessed December 27, 2012, http://www.ccv.org/wp-content/uploads/2010/04/Judith_Reisman_Senate_Testimony-2004.11.18.pdf.

[12] Covenant Eyes, *Pornography Statistics*, 8, https://www.bevillandassociates.com/wp-content/uploads/2015/05/2015-porn-stats-covenant-eyes-1.pdf.

[13] Anonymous, "National Review: Getting Serious On Pornography," NPR, March 31, 2010, https://www.npr.org/2010/03/31/125382361/national-review-getting-serious-on-pornography#:~:text=This%20finding%20is%20substantiated%20by,divorce%20cases%20the%20prior%20year.

According to a 2010 study by the National Coalition for the Protection of Children and Families, 47 percent of families in the United States reported that pornography is a problem in their home. Nearly 90 percent of children and teens say that no one in their lives is helping them avoid pornography, and 54 percent of those said they couldn't even think of anyone who could help them.[14]

* * *

In summary, it should be clear from what we have said that pornography is a monumental destroyer of marriage. It is terribly wrong, and terribly harmful to marriage and to all who are involved with it. Mike's story should make it clear that no matter how deeply addicted a person is, there is hope, through prayer, counseling, 12-step groups, and good, Christian friendships. Pornography kills marriages because it kills love. A loveless marriage is a nightmare.

---

[14] Family Research Council, "Pornography: America's Public Health Crisis," August 15, 2018, https://www.frc.org/blog/2018/08/pornography-americas-public-health-crisis.

CHAPTER XII

Children: Have Some!

THE FACT THAT MARRIAGE AND ITS form, conjugal love, are ordered to having and nurturing children is found in the very word *matrimony*. This contains two Latin words, the prefix *matri-*, meaning "mother," and *munus*, meaning "mission." So, marriage is the mission of motherhood (and fatherhood). Marriage is about a husband and wife loving each other so much that their love overflows into bringing forth children, who are its greatest crown and who will be a witness to that marital love for all eternity.

THE GIFT OF CHILDREN

As we saw above, Vatican II spoke glowingly about the blessing of children: "Children are really the supreme gift of marriage and contribute very much to the good of their parents."[1] Further on it states,

> As living members of the family, children contribute in their own way to the sanctification of their parents. For they will respond to the benefits given by their parents with sentiments of gratitude, with love and trust. They will help them as children customarily do, in hard times and in the loneliness of their old age.[2]

And, finally (as we saw above),

---

[1] Vatican II, *Gaudium et Spes*, nn. 48, 50. Translations are mine.
[2] Ibid., 48.

> Thus, trusting in divine Providence and culti-
> vating the spirit of sacrifice, Christian spouses
> glorify the Creator and strive toward perfection
> in Christ, when with generous human and
> Christian responsibility they carry out the duty
> to procreate. Among spouses who fulfill in
> this way their God-given mission, particular
> mention should be made of those who, after
> wise and common deliberation, generously
> undertake to bring up suitably even a rela-
> tively large number of children.[3]

So, children contribute to the good, and indeed, the
sanctification of their parents; they show their parents
gratitude, love, and trust for their kindness; they help
their parents in their old age. Parents, by fulfilling their
mission of having children, glorify God and grow in
perfection; and thus, parents who generously bring
forth and educate a large number of children are to
be given recognition.[4]

Pope John Paul II also spoke of the precious gift
of children:

> In its most profound reality, love is essen-
> tially a gift; and conjugal love, while leading
> the spouses to the reciprocal "knowledge"
> which makes them "one flesh," does not
> end with the couple, because it makes them
> capable of the greatest possible gift, the gift
> by which they become cooperators with God
> for giving life to a new human person. Thus
> the couple, while giving themselves to one
> another, give not just themselves but also the

---

[3] Ibid., 50.

[4] All of these elements go to make up what I would call the
"personalist" value of having children, something that was often
overlooked before Vatican II. Some theologians, alas, were calling
having children a "biological end of marriage."

reality of children, who are a living reflection of their love, a permanent sign of conjugal unity and a living and inseparable synthesis of their being a father and a mother.[5]

We might add to the above list of benefits for parents in having children the following. Children, in their early helplessness, draw parents out and beyond themselves to love them, and to achieve their fulfillment as parents and educators. Children are often new and special friends for the parents. Children, by their very existence, give witness to the love between husband and wife for all eternity (as the Holy Father pointed out). Children are a source of deepening spousal friendship since they are a common interest that draws husband and wife together. Children often form a link between the parents and the community, thereby opening new horizons for friendships.

Pope Paul VI also has some beautiful words about children:

> In love there is infinitely more than love. We would say that in human love there is divine love. And that is why the link between love and fecundity is deep, hidden, and substantial! All authentic love between a man and a woman, when it is not egoistic love, tends toward creation of another being issuing from that love. To love can mean "to love oneself," and often love is no more than the juxtaposition of two solitudes. But when one has passed beyond that stage of egoism, when one has truly understood that love is shared joy, a mutual gift, then one comes to what is *truly* love. If it is true that love is what I tell you it is, one can understand that it cannot

---

[5] *Familiaris Consortio*, n. 14.

be separated from the fruit of love. Even Plato taught us that love's spring is in the generation of souls in beauty, for the education of spirits. Love reaches out toward fecundity. It imitates the creative act. It renews. It gives life, it is a sacrifice on behalf of life.[6]

And from St. John Paul II again, "Human life is precious because it is the gift of a God whose love is infinite; and when God gives life, it is forever."[7]

Sacred Scripture has some wonderful things to say about having children:

> Sons are indeed a heritage from the Lord,
>   the fruit of the womb a reward.
> Like arrows in the hand of a warrior
>   are the sons of one's youth.
> Happy is the man who has
>   his quiver full of them.
> He shall not be put to shame
>   when he speaks with his enemies in the
>   gate. (Ps 127:3–5)

> God blessed [Adam and Eve] and God said to them, "Be fruitful and multiply, and fill the earth and subdue it . . ." (Gn 1:28)

The Catechism of the Catholic Church teaches, "Holy Scripture and the traditional practice of the Church see in large families a sign of the blessing of God and of the generosity of the parents."[8]

---

[6] Quoted in Jean Guitton, *The Pope Speaks: Dialogues of Paul VI with Jean Guitton*, trans. Anne and Christopher Fremantle (New York: Meredith Press, 1968), 275–76.

[7] John Paul II, "Holy Mass at the Capital Mall, Homily of His Holiness John Paul II," October 7, 1979, https://www.vatican.va/content/john-paul-ii/en/homilies/1979/documents/hf_jp-ii_hom_19791007_usa-washington.html.

[8] *Catechism of the Catholic Church* (Huntington, IN: Our Sunday Visitor, 2023), para. 2373.

LARGE FAMILY BENEFITS

Upon searching "benefits of large families" on the internet, I was surprised to see a good number of articles on the subject, including one from the *New York Times*.[9] Some of their points:

> (1) Children learn how to share. (2) They learn how to get along with others (better social skills). (3) They learn gratitude (without having a lot). (4) They entertain each other. (5) They learn to pitch in for the family. (6) They are never lonely (nor are their parents).[10]

So how many children should a devout Catholic have? They should have as many as they *reasonably* can, generously. The founder of *Opus Dei* was a great promoter of large families.

> St. Josemaria Escrivá was constant in his defense of [large] families, which he saw as the natural expression and support of conjugal love and of trust in God's fatherly providence, as well as the place where children themselves learn tolerance, mutual help, service and generosity, and so acquire the qualities that can keep social life human.[11]

So, as you think about bringing forth children for God in your marriage, think not so much about what they will cost you, but how they will enrich you and their siblings, and the blessings they will bring to you

---

[9] Laura Vanderkam, "What Everyone Can Learn from Parents of Big Families," *New York Times*, April 16, 2020, https://www.nytimes.com/2020/04/16/parenting/big-families.html.

[10] Based in part on Kathie Morrissey, "Advantages of Being Part of a Big Family," *My Joy-Filled Life*, https://www.myjoyfilledlife.com/advantages-part-big-family/.

[11] Cormac Burke, "Love and the Family in Today's World," *Homiletic & Pastoral Review*, March 1995, https://www.ewtn.com/catholicism/library/love-and-the-family-in-todays-world-11243.

and the world. And, in keeping with reason, try for lots of these blessings.

POPULATION EXPLOSION?

"But," you may ask, "what about the population explosion?" Many years ago, Julian Simon, professor of business administration at the University of Maryland, began to research this so-called "population explosion" problem.[12] Let's hear his story:

> Ironically, when I started to work on population studies, I assumed that the accepted view was sound. I aimed to help the world contain its "exploding" population. . . . But my reading and research led me into confusion. Though the then standard economic theory of population . . . asserted that a higher population growth implies a lower standard of living, the available empirical data did not support that theory. My technical 1977 book . . . arrived at a theory implying that population growth has positive economic effects in the long run, although there are costs in the short run.[13]

The conclusion of his voluminous book quoted above? People, and human intelligence, are the best resource we have, not oil or copper or any other natural resource. A population that slowly increases is best for

---

[12] Julian Simon, who died in 1998, was a senior fellow at the Cato Institute. *Fortune Magazine* named him one of the 150 Great Minds of the 1990s. He was a graduate of Harvard University and held a PhD in business from the University of Chicago. In 1980 Simon offered to bet anyone who would, that any basic commodity (wheat, oil, metals, whatever) would be cheaper ten years later. Population alarmist Paul Erlich made the bet, choosing copper, chrome, nickel, tin, and tungsten. Each of them dropped dramatically in price. Erlich had to pay. Simon's point was that people find, produce, and create more resources than they use.

[13] Julian Simon, *The Ultimate Resource II* (Princeton: Princeton University Press, 1996), xxxi.

economic growth. He claimed that reducing population growth is not the way to increase affluence, but vice versa. Helping countries to develop and have more affluence is the way to reduce excessive population growth.[14]

In 1999 business consultant Peter Drucker wrote, "the most important single new certainty—if only because there is no precedent for it in all of history—is the collapsing birthrate in the developed world."[15] As of 2021 the birthrate in western Europe was about 1.61 children per fertile couple, well below the replacement level of 2.1.[16] The birthrate in the US in 2021 was just under 1.8,[17] still under the replacement level, but one of the highest in a developed country. Thus, if there is a population problem in the developed world, it's not one of *over*-population.

EDUCATION COSTS FOR A LARGE FAMILY

When we brought up the issue of having a large family in our couples group, the question arose (more than once), "If we have a large number of children, how will we be able to pay for Catholic schooling?" Excellent question.

One of our couples that has nine children stepped up with their own witness on this. They pointed out

[14] In the nineties, Danish statistician Bjorn Lomborg read an article by Simon, in which he asserts that the prophets of doom were wrong. Lomborg became convinced that Simon was just some right-wing propagandist, and he brought together some of his smartest students to prove it. Much to their surprise, they discovered that the facts supported Simon! Lomborg published his research in *The Skeptical Environmentalist: Measuring The Real State of The World* (New York: Cambridge University Press, 2001).

[15] Peter F. Drucker, *Management Challenges for The 21st Century* (New York: Harper Collins, 1999), 44.

[16] Eurostat, "Fertility Statistics," March 6, 2024, https://ec.europa.eu/eurostat/statistics-explained.

[17] Macrotrends, "U. S. Fertility Rate 1950–2024," 2024, https://www.macrotrends.net/countries/USA/united-states/fertility-rate.

that they were able to make an offer to the Catholic schools their children attended, and the offer (quite a bit lower than the going rate) was almost always accepted. They had sent them all to good Catholic schools at a considerable discount because they had a large family. It seems that those with one or two children, by paying full tuition, in effect are helping those with larger families to pay less.

"WE'RE GOING TO WAIT A WHILE"

Years ago I was preparing a couple for marriage. She was thirty-four and he was thirty-six. The wife-to-be told me, "We're going to use natural family planning when we get married for the first few months. It may interfere with our honeymoon."

"Are you serious?" I asked. "You're thirty-four years old. You may not be able to have children if you wait."

"We're only going to wait a few months."

"Why do you want to wait?" I asked.

"Well, we want to get settled for a while first," she replied.

"But marriage is 'ordained to the procreation and education of children,' as Vatican II put it. Look, God knows how much time you need to get settled. You should be spontaneous in your love-making when you first marry, especially on your honeymoon. Why not let God help you with this?" I asked her.

"You mean we should give control to God here?"

"Sure. You're only going to have so many chances to have children at your age. You want to have three or more if you can, don't you?"

"Oh yes. We sure do. Well, let me talk it over with Melvin."

They did talk it over and decided not to be so

controlling. They left themselves open right from the honeymoon. In fact, they got pregnant on the honeymoon. And they were very happy they did.

Another couple was thinking of waiting because they were going to move in nine months. After some discussion, however, they decided that early openness to children might be more important than having a comfortable move. They, too, got pregnant on the honeymoon. Here's what the wife wrote me later:

> Because of our ages we decided to try for a family immediately, and God blessed us: I became pregnant three weeks after the wedding. To the "world" our decision might have seemed foolish. We were newly married, and living on a Navy salary. My husband was planning to leave the Navy in seven months and had no job lined up. However, God's ways are not our ways.
>
> Having a child immediately was the biggest blessing for our marriage. We moved to another state for Eldon's new job when I was 7½ months pregnant, and six weeks later Patrick was born. Our new baby brought us closer together right from the start. We focused together on our son, and that helped us bond as a couple. And, having a baby made it easy for us to meet people in our new environment.
>
> And, because we had a child so soon, we never fell into the trap of selfishness with our time or money. So many couples look back wistfully on the time before they had children, when they were free to travel and to spend more on their pleasures. We never had that period, so we have never missed it.
>
> By having a child right away, we imitated the Holy Family, and the Trinity. What could be more enriching than to turn two into three?

Thank you Suzy (who is a convert to Catholicism), for your great witness.

There are any number of reasons couples give for "waiting to have a baby." Many are reasons for not getting married yet. For example, "We want to get to know each other first." But, not only should a couple know each other *really well* before getting married, but having children, a common interest, helps people to know each other and to exercise self-giving love. We don't get to know our spouses by gazing into their eyes and absorbing their beauty—exterior and interior—in an *égoïsme á deux*, but by allowing our love for them to overflow into new life, imitating God's creative act. That is a true love, which is so strong that we don't selfishly keep it for ourselves, but share it with others.

I urge married couples to keep in mind these wonderful words from Vatican II cited earlier: ". . . the very institution of marriage and conjugal love, are ordained to the procreation and education of children and it is in them that they are crowned as by their summit."[18] In other words, the very love of husband and wife tends toward overflowing into children, who ". . . are really the supreme gift of marriage and contribute very much to the good of their parents."[19]

So, please be serenely open to children *early* in your marriage. Those I know who have done so are happy they did.

WHEN CHILDREN DON'T COME EASILY

Attorneys Anthony and Stephanie Epolite married in their late thirties, and after trying for some time to have a baby, they were deeply disappointed. When

---

[18] *Gaudium et Spes*, n. 48.
[19] Ibid., 50.

Stephanie was approaching her thirty-ninth birthday without any prospect for conceiving, they went to see their doctor. He referred them to a fertility clinic. When they asked their parish priest about pursuing in vitro fertilization (IVF) he told them, "Do whatever you feel comfortable with." (Pray for that man!)[20]

So, off they went. They met with a doctor who did no tests, took no blood, and seemed very cold, very matter of fact. He told them that IVF was their only option, what with Stephanie about to turn thirty-nine. Next, they met with a kind of salesperson to decide which "package" they wanted: one cycle, two, or three. They weren't warming up to this whole thing, but it seemed like their last hope, so they forged ahead.

They would surgically remove several ova (eggs) from Stephanie and then introduce a sperm cell from Anthony in a petri dish. They would observe under a microscope to see if fertilization occurred. If it did, she would be invited back in to have the embryo inserted into her womb. For two cycles of work, the price was a cool $25,000, with no guarantee that there would even be a fertilization. During the two months of preparation, Anthony had to inject his wife with several drugs in different parts of her body.

When they completed their part of the procedure, they went home to await the call. The only call they got was to tell them it didn't work. The comment at the end of the consultation was "You will probably never have a family." And, of course, the $25,000 was down the drain. (For more on the problems of IVF, see Appendix B.)

---

[20] Most of this is based on Chuck Weber, "Agents of Change," *Catholic Culture*, https://www.catholicculture.org/culture/library/view.cfm?recnum=6669.

NAPRO TO THE RESCUE

In 2001 Stephanie called a longtime friend who was a certified instructor and practitioner in the Creighton Model FertilityCare System, a natural family planning method developed by Dr. Thomas Hilgers at Creighton University in Omaha, Nebraska. Stephanie's friend was well qualified in natural procreative (NaPro) technology. Right away her friend taught Stephanie how to chart her fertility signs. This data would be analyzed by a NaPro doctor to determine just what was keeping the Epolites from getting pregnant.

According to Dr. Hilgers, developer of the NaPro method at the Paul VI Institute for the Study of Human Reproduction, "Most medical approaches today bypass the woman's problem or simply override her natural processes altogether. With NaPro we find out *why* the body is not functioning correctly, then apply treatments that work cooperatively with the body."[21]

Once the doctor evaluates the data and discovers the problems, he can use one of the state-of-the-art medical procedures spelled out in Dr. Hilgers's 1300-page book, *Medical and Surgical Practice of NaPro Technology.*[22] In it, Dr. Hilgers explains some key advances in dealing with endometriosis,[23] polycystic ovarian disease, blocked fallopian tubes, and hormonal disorders. These are often some of the problems that underlie infertility.

---

[21] Ibid.

[22] Thomas W. Hilgers, *Medical and Surgical Practice of NaPro Technology* (Omaha, NE: Pope Paul VI Institute Press, 2004).

[23] With endometriosis, cells that normally grow inside the uterus (womb), grow outside it. It may or may not cause pain and infertility. Endometriosis is one of the most common causes of female infertility. The American Society for Reproductive Medicine found that 24 to 50 percent of women dealing with infertility have endometriosis. See https://www.hopkinsmedicine.org/health/conditions-and-diseases/endometriosis.

Once the Epolites had sent in their data, they went out to Omaha, to the Paul VI Institute, and they found it anything but the cold, impersonal environment of the artificial insemination clinic. The people treated them with, "respect, kindness, compassion, and love." It was July 2001. They had been getting Stephanie's blood samples for several months in clinics near their home. In Omaha, Dr. Hilgers had some diagnostic tests done and determined that she suffered from endometriosis and blocked fallopian tubes. Anthony's sperm count was discovered to be low.

During their two weeks in Omaha, doctors performed NaPro surgery on Stephanie, and Anthony was given a list of nutritional supplements to take. They waited and waited. It seemed like forever. When they were invited to speak at a natural family planning conference in March 2002 about their IVF fiasco, they agreed, but were not enthusiastic about it, since they had yet to find success by this other, new approach.

By the time they got to the conference, however, they had more than their IVF misadventure to report: Stephanie announced that they were seven weeks pregnant! They received a tearful standing ovation.

On October 31, 2002, Claire Marie Epolite was born. NaPro had succeeded where IVF had failed.

(For more on the many successes of NaPro healing a number of different medical problems, see Appendix C.)

There is a growing number of NaPro doctors available throughout the country. To find one, just go to https://www.fertilitycare.org/AA/find-a-center and click on your state, or call the Pope Paul VI Institute at (402) 390-6600.

CHAPTER XIII
Catholic Couples Groups

C ANA CLUBS FOR CATHOLIC MARRIED couples were quite popular in the 1950s and 1960s. When *Humanae Vitae* came out and so many dissented from the Church's teaching on contraception, Cana clubs began to disappear. Couples did not need support groups to live as the world lives.

In 1984 I began a couples group that we called the John Paul II Cana Club. John Paul II was in the title to make it clear that we were going to be faithful to ALL the teachings of the Church. In fact, the first material we discussed was *Familiaris Consortio*, John Paul II's exhortation on the family. We met monthly in couples' homes, having dinner first, then praying the rosary with meditations, and then discussing the faith. We would meet Saturday or Sunday evenings. Couples have told me that they love coming to these meetings because they know they can talk freely about the faith and find support for living it. For many it has been a "delightful night out together."

Since then I started several other groups for couples, and as of this writing I have had two groups meeting regularly. It is a great blessing for me, a celibate priest, since I am able to participate in some way in their family life. I get many ideas for preaching topics based on our discussions. I also discover ideas on how to help couples in trouble.

It quickly became a kind of book club. We studied such books as *The Dialogue of St. Catherine of Siena,*

The Life of Christ by Bishop Fulton Sheen, two books on marriage by Gary Smalley (*If Only He Knew* for men and *For Better or for Best* for women), *Covenant of Love* by Hogan and LeVoir, *The Theology of The Body* by Pope John Paul II, and *The Blessing* by Gary Smalley on raising good children, to name a few. We read these books aloud at the meetings (I tried to avoid homework for the couples). We also viewed several hours of Mark Gungor's *Laughing Your Way to A Better Marriage*[1] (spread over nine months). And we watched movies like *Fireproof, Facing the Giants, Flywheel,* and *Courageous.*

We followed two possible arrangements for dinner. One group provided pizza and drinks each month with the couples contributing to the host couple for the cost. The other group was a bit of a potluck. There have been some great meals with both groups.

There are other groups of Catholic couples in the Church, for example, Teams of Our Lady.[2] They were founded in Paris, France in 1939 by a Father Caffarel and four married couples. In 1947 they were formally established under the name "Equipes Notre Dame." In 1992, the Pontifical Council for the Laity recognized them as an international association of the faithful. Teams of Our Lady came to the United States in 1958 and are now found all across the country. I became involved in a Teams group in 2018 and have loved it.

---

[1] Gungor has some great insights into marriage, but with two significant flaws. First, he suggests a man should love his wife to get more sex. In fact, a man should love his wife because he vowed to do so at his wedding. Secondly, he is skittish about unconditional love, understood as benevolence toward the spouse, regardless of his/her behavior. This is essential to a good marriage.

[2] See https://members.teamsofourlady.org/about_us_1.

Each couple is encouraged to commit to the "endeavors" of the Teams group. These are:

- Listen regularly to the Word of God. Read Sacred Scripture daily and reflect upon it.
- Turn to God daily in silent prayer (personal prayer).
- Pray together daily as a couple (conjugal prayer) and if possible with the children (family prayer). This would include the Magnificat, which is the official prayer of the Teams. The rosary would appear to be a good way to fulfill that endeavor.
- Make time each month for true dialogue together: the "sit-down." It is suggested that this begin with prayer to seek guidance in talking about things each person has in his/her heart.
- Choose some specific points of personal effort: the "rule of life." Each should pursue one or two things to improve their relationship with the Lord and each other.
- Make an annual retreat.

Attendance at the meetings is obligatory, barring serious difficulties. (Not a bad idea, since these meetings are very important for the couples.) I encourage our couples to keep in mind that when they attend a meeting they are not only finding support for their own marriages, but ministering to the other couples as well.

In summary, attending couples groups such as Teams of Our Lady is a great way to receive and provide support for living a truly Catholic marriage. Find a solid priest and start such a group!

The Theology
of the Body[1]

I
T SEEMS THAT POPE JOHN PAUL II'S
Theology of the Body was an answer to the arguments of dissenters from *Humanae Vitae*, not to
mention those of contemporary philosophers. The
dissenters claimed that saying contraception, or any
other bodily act, was immoral was "physicalism," that
is, allowing the physical structure of the person to
determine the morality of his acts. In fact, the dissenters, in their arguments, fell into the opposite
extreme—that of dualism. Dualism is the belief that
only the spiritual counts; the physical is of no significance. The Catholic view is that both the physical and
spiritual are important, but the spiritual is primary.

So Pope John Paul II gave a series of talks about
the "Theology of the Body" from 1979 to 1984 in
his Wednesday audiences, in which he spelled out
the importance of the body and the beautiful love
language it expresses, especially within marriage.
He spoke of the nuptial meaning of the body, and
the fact that man must feel the call to redemption,
a call to once again see the spousal meaning of the
body and to put forth the freedom that comes from
self-mastery. The original power stemming from

---

[1] In this appendix, the reader is encouraged to wade through
the presentation of the thought of Pope St. John Paul II, until
the summary of each section, which attempts to make clear the
application of his thought.

creation is fulfilled in the grace of redemption.[2]

Redemption enables us to rediscover the person, with all his/her values, as someone to be loved, not to be seen as merely an object of enjoyment.

The "new man" can come forth when the ethos (way of behavior) of the redemption of the body "dominates the concupiscence [disordered appetite] of the flesh and the whole man of concupiscence.... Redemption contains ... the imperative of self-mastery, the necessity of immediate continence [self-control] and habitual temperance."[3] With regard to sexual desires, this "habitual temperance" is chastity. Chastity is the habit of sexual sobriety, sexual purity.

The Holy Father considered six main topics:

1. The Beginning
2. The Redemption of the Heart
3. The Resurrection of the Flesh
4. Christian Virginity (which we will omit since it does not apply to our main interest, marriage)
5. Christian Marriage
6. Love and Fruitfulness

THE BEGINNING

When the Jews challenged Jesus's declaration that divorce was unacceptable (Mt 19:3ff) he refers to "the beginning" to establish the truth of his declaration. In other words, the story of Genesis is normative for understanding mankind.[4]

---

[2] John Paul II, *Man and Woman He Created Them: A Theology of the Body*, trans. Michael Waldstein (Boston: Pauline Books & Media, 2006), 313.
[3] Ibid., 324.
[4] Ibid., 131–33.

In Genesis we find the "*boundary... between man's primeval innocence and original sin.*" Man's original innocence is indicated by the sentence, "Now both were naked, the man and his wife, but they did not feel shame" (Gn 2:25).[5]

Immediately after this comes the fall of man, original sin. Man moves from the "state of integral nature" to the "state of fallen nature."[6] Yet in the third chapter of Genesis will come the *Protoevangelium*, the "first good news," of a savior who will crush the head of the serpent. Thus, mankind lives in anticipation of the redemption; he "*participates in the history of salvation.*" This redemption will include, as St. Paul said, "the redemption of our bodies" (Rom 8:23). "... This *perspective of the redemption of the body guarantees the continuity and the unity* between man's hereditary state of sin and his original innocence, although within history this innocence has been [irretrievably] lost by him."[7]

Original Solitude

John Paul II considers the meaning of original solitude spoken of in Genesis: "It is not good that the man should be alone; I will make a suitable partner for him" (Gn 2:18). He tells us man is different in two senses, one based on his human nature—as different from that of the animals—and the other based on the "*relationship between male and female.*" The Lord formed all the animals and brought them to the man to name, "but the man did not find a helper similar to himself" among them (Gn 2:20). He has knowledge

---

5 Ibid., 140.
6 Ibid., 140–41.
7 Ibid., 143–44.

of himself, an indication of his humanity, and realizes
he is a "person."[8]

In cautioning the man not to eat of "the fruit of
the tree of the knowledge of good and evil" (Gn 2:17),
God shows man to be capable of "choice and self-
determination" (as well as self-consciousness, which
his sense of being alone indicated).[9]

Pope John Paul II goes even further to say that
man discovers that his body provides him with the
capacity to perform human activity. As such, "the body
expresses the person."[10]

This is essential to understand the theology of the
body: the body is in no way extrinsic to the person;
it communicates the person, makes him known. It
expresses who he is. Thus, John Paul II undermines
the dualistic error held by dissenting theologians,
that the body is somehow peripheral to the person,
separated from his spirit. What we do with our bodies is critical to our moral character. The comment
of a movie star that her sexual involvement with a
male friend was just a "silly little affair" flies in the
face of reality.

Original Unity

Subsequently, in the Genesis account, God will
produce the woman, and indicate the unity intended
between her and the man by the words, "A man will
leave his father and his mother and unite with his
wife, and the two will be one flesh" (Gn 2:24). John
Paul II adds that man's being a body is more fundamental to his personhood than the fact that he

---

[8] Ibid., 147–48, 150.
[9] Ibid., 151.
[10] Ibid., 154.

is male or female. Thus, original solitude precedes original unity.[11]

In his original solitude, man is personally conscious of his difference from the animals, but this also opens him to a "helper similar to himself." This opening prepares him for the possibility of a *communio personarum*, a communion of persons, with the woman.[12]

If we go back to the first account of the creation of man found in chapter one of Genesis, we find that man and woman together were created in the image of God (Gn 1:27). From this we can deduce that *"man became the image of God not only through his own humanity, but also through the communion of persons*, which man and woman form from the very beginning." Mankind images, in the original unity of man and woman in marriage, "an [incomprehensible] divine communion of Persons," namely, the Trinity.[13]

To be sure, the unity of "one flesh" is the conjugal act, the sexual intimacy of husband and wife. This union is based on the choice each has made of the other. This conjugal union *"carries within itself a particular awareness of the meaning of [the] body in the reciprocal self-gift of the persons."* In rediscovering the awareness of the unitive meaning of the body in each marital act, this union "renews in some way the mystery of creation in all its original depth and vital power."[14]

In other words, when a man has sexual relations with his wife, he symbolizes the beauty of uniting profoundly with another, an intimacy that in some way reflects the intimacy of the three divine persons.

---

[11] Ibid., 157.
[12] Ibid., 162.
[13] Ibid., 163.
[14] Ibid., 167–69.

Original Nakedness

Genesis states, "Now both were naked, the man and his wife, but they did not feel shame" (Gn 2:25). After the original sin, this changes: "Then the eyes of both were opened and they realized that they were naked; they sewed fig leaves together and made themselves loincloths." John Paul II calls this a "boundary" or "threshold" experience. They moved from having no shame to a state of shame.[15]

He points out that the lack of shame speaks actually not of a lack but of a "ful[l]ness of consciousness and experience, above all the ful[l]ness of understanding the meaning of the body . . ." Their absence of shame indicates "an original depth in affirming what is inherent in the person . . . through which the 'personal intimacy' of reciprocal communication is constituted in all its radical simplicity and purity." In their shame-free encounter, they have an "*'interior' ful[l]ness of the vision of man in God* . . ."[16] They see each other as God sees them, as a person in their lofty dignity. They see each other with the peace of the "interior gaze," which brings personal intimacy.[17]

In other words, man and woman are able to see each other in their personal fullness as they were before the fall, as opposed to only seeing each other as they were after. A spontaneous personal intimacy is possible.

The Gift

The pope proclaims that creation involves the most basic and first gift, or gifts. Man receives existence; man has received the world; the world has received

---

[15] Ibid., 170–72.
[16] Ibid., 174, 176.
[17] Ibid., 178.

him; he has received the woman. All are gifts from God.[18] The biblical words "alone" and "help" speak of the essence of personhood: to live in communion with another or others. Man is fulfilled by living "for" another and having the other do the same, by living "in a relationship of reciprocal gift."[19]

"The body, which expresses femininity 'for' masculinity, and vice versa . . . manifests the reciprocity and the communion of persons. It expresses it through gift as the fundamental characteristic of personal existence." The two are naked without shame and thus each is free to give himself to, and receive, the other in unselfish love, the love that "fulfills the very meaning of his being and existence." This is the living out of the fundamental teaching of Vatican II: ". . . man, who is the only creature on earth which God willed for its own sake, cannot fully find himself except through a sincere gift of self." This so-called "interior freedom of the gift" enables the man and woman to give themselves unselfishly to each other. And each can receive the other as a person willed "for its own sake."[20]

In other words, he welcomes her for her sake, for her good, not his own, and vice versa. And, paradoxically, in so doing, he "finds himself," or fulfills himself, as does she.[21] Christ intimated this in Matthew 10:39: ". . . he who loses his life for my sake will find it." In this sense, in original innocence resulting from grace, the body has a full "spousal" meaning.[22]

After the fall, the interior gaze which made loving the other person selflessly natural, was no longer a

---

18 Ibid., 180–81.
19 Ibid., 182.
20 Ibid., 185–87.
21 Ibid., 197.
22 Ibid., 190, 192.

given. It is as if a man no longer sees a woman in her totality, with all her values together, including her sexual values. Rather, in his fallen state, the man sees only her exterior values, her physical or sexual values, with the others obscured. To have true unity with the woman, he must strive to recover that vision by grace and return to loving the other for her sake.[23]

Marriage then, in the beginning, was the original sacrament (or *sign*) manifesting the mystery in God, the divine *communion of persons*. And it is in the body, or bodies, that this mystery is made known.

Knowledge and Procreation

In Genesis chapter four, we read that Adam *knew* his wife and she gave birth to a son. The union in one flesh is thus raised to a deeper personal level. In "knowing" each other the sacred text "indicated the deepest essence of reality of shared married life." They "reveal themselves to one another" in the depths of their being.[24]

And procreation enables the two to "*know each other reciprocally in the 'third,' originated by both.*" The woman proclaims, "I have acquired a man from the Lord" (Gn 4:1). As such, she manifests "*awareness of the mystery of creation, which renews itself in human generation,*" and knowledge of God's involvement in this process.[25]

The man and his wife share in the mystery of creation by bringing forth, with God, a new human person. This child will give a name to their loving union and give witness to that union for all eternity.

---

[23] Ibid., 202.
[24] Ibid., 206–7.
[25] Ibid., 211, 213.

Summary of *"the Beginning"*

When Jesus spoke of "the beginning," responding to the Pharisees' question about the permanence of marriage, he invited us to go to that beginning for an understanding of the body, and a theology of the body. It is there that we find the truth regarding an "integral vision of man" of which Paul VI spoke in *Humanae Vitae* (n. 7). "This truth *concerns the meaning of the human body in the structure of the personal subject.*" Pope John Paul II explained that it should be no surprise that theology should include the body. Once God became incarnate in Jesus Christ, "the body entered theology... through the main door." The Incarnation and the resulting redemption have become "the definitive source of the sacramentality of marriage."[26]

It seems that the Lord, in the redemption of the body, would have us recover human dignity in which "the true meaning of the body," as an expression of the person and of personal communion, is restored.[27]

In conclusion, then, Jesus's appeal to "the beginning" can be taken as an invitation to discover the original intent of the Creator for marriage and the body. The body is not just a physical appendage of the person, but an integral part of the person, a part that expresses the person. In the beginning man and woman were free to express their love in a way that reflected the divine love of God—for the other, not for the self. They were free to give themselves to each other because they had an "interior gaze" to see the whole person, body and soul, as someone worthy of love. The body had a "spousal meaning" because it could express true, unselfish married love. There is a theology of the body

---

[26] Ibid., 221.
[27] Ibid., 222.

because there is a theology of the person, and the body expresses that person.

THE REDEMPTION OF THE HEART

In this second segment of his talks, John Paul II takes on the passage from Matthew 5:27–28: "You have heard it said, 'you shall not commit adultery.' But I say to you: Whoever looks at a woman [lustfully] has already committed adultery with her *in his heart*." He says this passage is another key to understanding the theology of the body. Morality is not just avoiding certain behavior, but an interior condition of the heart. It is an appeal to the "inner man."[28]

Meaning of Original Shame

The First Letter of John also speaks of lust, or three-fold concupiscence: "All that is in the world, the con-cupiscence of the flesh, the concupiscence of the eyes, and the pride of life, comes not from the Father but from the world. And the world passes away with its concupiscence; but the one who does the will of God will remain in eternity" (1 Jn 2:16–17). John Paul II (JPII) points out that these three come from the world, "not as a fruit of the mystery of creation, but as a fruit of 'the tree of the knowledge of good and evil.'" In other words, they come from the fallen world. The Holy Father links this with the experience of shame mentioned in Genesis. The Adam who experienced shame is the Adam of concupiscence.[29]

It seems the fear of his own nakedness implies a "radical change" in the man. "*Man in some way loses the original certainty of the 'image of God' expressed in his*

---

[28] Ibid., 225, 227–29.
[29] Ibid., 234–35, 238.

body. He also loses in a certain way the sense of his right *to participate in the perception of the world*, which he enjoyed in the mystery of creation." He has lost that "divine vision" of the world he had in the beginning, including the original acceptance of the body as an expression of the person. Implied as well, as manifested by the words of Genesis 3:17–19 ("Cursed is the ground because of you; in toil you shall eat of it . . . "), is a breach in his harmony with the material world.[30] In his fallen state, "the body is not subject to the spirit as in the state of original innocence." There is rather a rebellion of the body against the spirit and his moral unity is thereby threatened.[31] This disordered appetite is concupiscence.

Insatiability of the Union

In addition, the original communion between the man and woman, symbolized by the peace they experienced in their nakedness, is "overturned." The ease of communion is lost. It is no longer a simple, spontaneous thing. The *"power of a full reciprocal communion"* has ceased.[32] JPII asks rhetorically if the visual concupiscence does not make the other an object of use?[33] Persons become aware of the "insatiability" of their union.[34] In other words, a superficial union based on use cannot satisfy the human heart.

> . . . *The communion of persons*—which consists in the spiritual unity of the two subjects who gave themselves to each other—*is replaced by a different mutual relationship*, namely by

---

[30] Ibid., 241–42.
[31] Ibid., 244.
[32] Ibid., 247–48.
[33] Ibid., 252.
[34] Ibid., 253.

a relationship *of possession* of the other as an object of one's desire."[35]

As such there is a "deformation of the spousal meaning of the body."[36]

Eros, the desire for the good, the beautiful, and the true in the other, tends to dominate. The man becomes more interested in fulfilling this desire than in pursuing the good of his wife. Paradoxically, subordinating his desire for her values to a desire to serve her good, and to make her life better, brings about fulfillment for him *and* his wife.

Gospel Ethical System (Ethos)

Jesus came to establish a new ethos, or ethical norm, for his people, which he preached during the Sermon on the Mount.[37] The people had compromised the law promoted by the prophets (such as Hosea and Ezekiel) which Jesus came to fulfill.[38] The new ethos of the Gospel moves the *"meaning of adultery from the 'body' to the 'heart.'"*[39]

The Heart of the Man of Concupiscence

John Paul II points out, using Sirach (23:17–22) that the man who wants to satisfy his senses doesn't find himself, but rather *"consumes himself."* By dismissing conscience his passion "wears itself out," it "exhausts itself." He detaches himself from the spousal meaning of the body, which is the foundation of the communion of persons.[40]

---

[35] Ibid., 254.
[36] Ibid., 256.
[37] Ibid., 264.
[38] Ibid., 274–75.
[39] Ibid., 279.
[40] Ibid., 284–86.

Concupiscence clouds the rich array of values another possesses and reduces that other person to her sexual value. Seeing a woman with her value of sex as part of her rich store of values is good. Reducing her to merely her sexual value, as an object of his pleasure, is not.[41]

John Paul II relates all this to the "purity of heart" called for in the Beatitudes. While recognizing that this purity has a "broad meaning" in Scripture, it includes the purity that underlies chastity.[42] In other words, purity of heart is not limited to the virtue of purity, but encompasses a single-mindedness, where God and the things of God are foremost in the heart of the believer.

The Holy Father distinguishes between a Manichaean dualistic viewpoint regarding the body and sex and the Christian viewpoint. For the former, the body and sexuality are in a sense an "anti-value," whereas for Christianity they are "a value not sufficiently appreciated." The words identifying "adultery of the heart" in Matthew are an "accusation," but even more so, says JPII, an "appeal." The appeal is *"to detach oneself from the evil of the act"* (concupiscence) and not *"transfer the negativity of this act to its object"* as would a Manichaean.[43] In other words, *it is not the body which is evil, but the misuse, or lustful viewing thereof.*

St. Margaret of Cortona wanted to destroy her beauty because she believed it had caused her to live a life of sin. Her spiritual director forbade her to do harm to her beauty. In fact, God revealed to her that

---

[41] Ibid., 287–88.
[42] Ibid., 300.
[43] Ibid., 307–8.

he wanted her to use her beauty to encourage sinners to convert. The cause of her sins was not her beauty, but her flawed heart.

The appeal of Christ is a call to redemption, a call, as we saw above, to once again see the spousal meaning of the body and to live in the freedom that comes from self-mastery. The original power stemming from creation is fulfilled in the grace of redemption.

> [This appeal of Christ] always signifies—even if only in the dimension of the act to which it refers—the rediscovery of the meaning of the whole of existence, of the meaning of life, which includes also the meaning of the body that we have called "spousal" here.[44]

> Man must not see himself as accused of a permanent concupiscence of the flesh, but rather called to the "supreme value, which is love." He is called in the truth of his humanity, of his body, his inheritance "of the beginning" which is more powerful than his inherited sinfulness, the threefold concupiscence in the Gospel of John.[45]

From Concupiscence to Temperance

The ethos of redemption must prevail over concupiscence. This begins with self-mastery (self-control) and ends with the full virtue of habitual temperance, chastity.[46] The former must govern until the value of chastity takes hold of the will and brings even the desires under the control of reason, thereby producing the peace of chastity. This provides him with "the freedom of the gift," whereby he can love and not exploit.

---

[44] Ibid., 313.
[45] Ibid., 314.
[46] Ibid., 324.

In other words, when a person has the virtue of chastity, he is so convinced, mind and heart, that unchaste activity will not make him happy that he is not even tempted to be unchaste. However, while he is developing this virtue, he needs self-control or self-mastery. With self-control there is a struggle, and he can win. With the full virtue of chastity there is no longer a struggle to be chaste. It follows with the conversion of the heart.

This new ethos is what St. Paul calls "living by the Spirit": "Live by the Spirit and do not satisfy the desires of the flesh; for the flesh has desires contrary to the Spirit, and the Spirit has desires contrary to the flesh; for these are opposed to each other so that you do not do what you want" (Gal 5:16–17). Paul speaks of the "fruit of the Spirit" and the "works of the flesh" (Gal 5:19–23). The latter are not all carnal sins, but include things such as idolatry, sorcery, strife, and jealousy. Thus these are more properly "sins of the human spirit."[47]

Paul goes on to say in Galatians, "For you were called to freedom, brothers; But do not use this freedom as an opportunity for the flesh; rather, serve one another through love. For the whole law is fulfilled in one statement, namely, 'You shall love your neighbor as yourself.'" (Gal 5:13–14). In other words, freedom must be subject to love, which is the highest value. Freedom is for love, not for selfishness.[48]

St. Paul doesn't mention purity as part of the fruit of the Spirit, but he does mention "self-mastery" or self-control. Inasmuch as he sets these fruits against such sins as fornication, impurity, licentiousness,

---

[47] Ibid., 336.
[48] Ibid., 339–40.

drunkenness, and orgies, it seems that he wants self-mastery to lead to temperance, the virtue that moderates all the appetites. This would appear to apply especially to chastity—temperance in the sexual realm.[49]

Purity as Virtue and Gift

In 1 Corinthians Paul again speaks of the need for purity.

> Shun fornication! Every sin that a person commits is outside the body; but the fornicator sins against the body itself. Or do you not know that your body is a temple of the Holy Spirit within you, which you have from God, and that you are not your own? (1 Cor 6:18–19)

The sin of fornication (*porneia* in Greek) is one that "profanes" the body, drags it down and is totally opposed to the reverence due to it in light of its personal dignity. But Paul goes further, saying that this body of ours deserves reverence not just because it is a person's but also because the Holy Spirit dwells within it. This is so due to the redemption won by Christ, a redemption that includes the body. The fact that Christ became man elevated mankind's dignity, and calls for "a new *measure of the holiness of the body*."[50] *Noblesse oblige!*

By analyzing the Scripture texts, the Holy Father says we discover a "theology of the body," which is an anthropology, a study of human nature. This is contrasted with the scientific view that the body is just an organism, rather than the manifestation, or sign, of the person. The theology of the body, on the other hand, can be seen as a "*spirituality of the body*."[51]

---

[49] Ibid., 341.
[50] Ibid., 349–51.
[51] Ibid., 361.

The pope then refers to the teaching of *Gaudium et Spes* in Vatican II, as it proclaims that conjugal love is often less than what it should be, due to, among other things, "egoism, hedonism, and illicit practices against generation."[52] Pope Paul VI remarked in *Humanae Vitae* that a man using contraception "may finally lose reverence for the woman and . . . may come to the point of considering her as a mere instrument of selfish enjoyment, and no longer as his respected and beloved companion."[53] This, says JPII, is just what we have been considering in the words of Jesus regarding the permanence of marriage, purity of heart, and mastery of the flesh, and the words of St. Paul on the redemption of the heart.[54]

Paul VI is quoted again as saying that self-denial is needed for the self-control in periodic continence (natural family planning). This discipline, he said, "favors attention to one's partner, helps both parties to drive out egoism, the enemy of true love, and deepens their sense of responsibility."[55] The theology of the body, based on Christ's teaching, is needed to understand these words of Paul VI and the Church's teaching on marriage in general.[56]

Summary of the Redemption of the Heart

Pope John Paul focused here on the "redemption of the heart" whereby man must purify his heart to live the spousal meaning of the body. The shame man experienced after the fall indicates a loss of the divine vision whereby he accepted the body as an

---

[52] *Gaudium et Spes*, n. 47.
[53] *Humanae Vitae*, n. 17.
[54] John Paul II, *Man and Woman*, 363.
[55] *Humanae Vitae*, n. 21.
[56] John Paul II, *Man and Woman*, 363.

expression of the person. Thus, the ease of communion is lost, prevented by seeing the other as an object of use. Christ calls us to a new ethical pattern (ethos) whereby mankind realizes the spousal meaning of the body in which he is free to give himself in love, and not to use others selfishly. The body should be treated with reverence since the Holy Spirit dwells within it. When Christ became man he brought forth a "new measure for holiness of the body." The theology of the body, which could be called a "spirituality of the body," is an anthropology that upholds the body as a manifestation of the person. This is over and against the ultra-scientific view that the body is just an organism.

When a man experiences the redemption of his heart, through the life of grace, he can embrace the truth about sex and the body. He can see clearly that sex is something special, indeed holy, and should never be trivialized; that he should love his wife, and thus never treat her (or anyone) as an object of use; that he is created in the image and likeness of God, and thus can live by reason, and not be controlled by his urges as are animals. As a redeemed man, the "new man," as St. Paul puts it, he can live at peace with his sexual appetite once it is trained in the new ethos of the Gospel.

With a redeemed heart a man can live in a communion of persons that is free of selfishness, free of concupiscence. He can live agapaic love that is focused above all on the good of the beloved. When this is the first dynamic in a marriage a profound intimacy is possible in the conjugal act, and in the common life of husband and wife.

A worthy manifestation of such intimacy is a chaste embrace. This is why marriage counselors often recommend frequent hugs for couples to manifest their intimate love relationship. A hug is a beautiful sign of solidarity, which affirms and strengthens their personal communion (as we saw in Chapter IV above).

RESURRECTION OF THE FLESH

Pope John Paul II next considers the passage in which the Sadducees presented this case, hoping to refute the concept of our resurrection:

> There were seven brothers; the first took a wife, and when he died left no children; and the second took her, and died, leaving no children; and the third likewise; and the seven left no children. Last of all the woman also died. In the resurrection whose wife will she be? For the seven had her as wife. (Mk 12:20–23)

Jesus answers that they are mistaken, since when people rise to new life, they do not marry. And, as God spoke of himself to Moses as the God of Abraham, Isaac, and Jacob, it should be clear that these three are living since he is God of the living, not of the dead.[57]

One of the points Jesus makes here is that marriage "belongs *exclusively to this world.*" Jesus's words that those who rise will "take neither wife nor husband" (Mk 12:25) indicate that they will still be male or female but not for the sake of marriage and procreation. The fact that they will "be like angels" indicates that the body will experience a "*spiritualization.*" This means that the spirit will master the body, but beyond that, will "*also fully permeate the body and the powers of the spirit will permeate the energies of the body.*" All conflict between body and spirit is eliminated.[58]

---

[57] Ibid., 381.
[58] Ibid., 387–89, 391.

The fact that those who rise will be "sons of God, being sons of the resurrection" (Lk 20:36) indicates that they will be "divinized" participating "in the divine nature, in the inner life of God himself . . . in a perfect communion of persons. This intimacy—with all its objective intensity—will not absorb man's personal subjectivity, but quite on the contrary, will make it emerge in an incomparably greater and fuller measure." In other words, the human person's unique personality will not be absorbed into God, but rather, it will be perfected in its own uniqueness.[59]

By our understanding of the fulfillment of the resurrected body in God, we can conclude that

> Marriage and procreation do not definitively determine the original and fundamental meaning of being a body, nor of being . . . male and female. Marriage and procreation only give concrete reality to that meaning in the dimensions of history. The resurrection indicates the closure of the historical dimension. . . . The spousal meaning of the body will be fulfilled in a way that is both "*personal* and *communitarian.*"[60]

The glorification of our human bodies will show forth the full meaning of the human body, which signified here on earth the created person, and made possible our self-communication to others by which we showed forth our personhood and love, thereby building up the communion of persons. In the next world, our glorified bodies will be made manifest with such "*simplicity and splendor*" that they will be the "fountain of the freedom of the gift." This gift will facilitate our love with all the saints in the Kingdom.[61]

---

[59] Ibid., 392–93.
[60] Ibid., 399.
[61] Ibid., 400.

Summary of the Resurrection of the Flesh

Our communion with God is the "fulfillment of human subjectivity and, on this basis, the definitive fulfillment of the 'spousal' meaning of the body." Christ's explanation of our state in the resurrection completes the "revelation of the body." It began with his teaching of what was "in the beginning" regarding the indissolubility of marriage and reached forward to this explanation of the resurrection. All three dimensions of man—these two (the beginning and the resurrection) plus the contemporary one—combine in establishing the theology of the body.[62]

We will not be without intimate communion with another in the Kingdom, but that communion will be with God. Scripture likens it to a marriage. For example, the Song of Songs is a rather long lyrical poem about the passionate love between husband and wife, seen by scholars as an allegory of the love between God and his people. We can read in Isaiah 62:5, "as the bridegroom rejoices over the bride, so shall your God rejoice over you." In Isaiah 54:5 we find, "Your Maker is your husband, the Lord of hosts is his name . . ." In Hosea 2:20 we find God taking back his *adulterous* lover Israel: "I will take you for my wife in faithfulness; and you shall know the Lord." In Ezekiel 16 the Lord addresses his people, Jerusalem, as his unfaithful spouse with whom he later restores his covenant. And in Revelation 19:7 there is rejoicing because "the marriage of the Lamb has come, and his bride has made herself ready," the Lamb being Jesus. And, finally, in Ephesians 5:25, "Husbands, love your wives, just as Christ loved the church and gave himself up for

---

[62] Ibid., 396–97.

her. . . ." (JPII will consider this passage in more detail in the next section.)

There is no doubt such passages as these inspired St. Gregory the Great to write, "The husband of every Christian soul is God; for she is joined to Him by faith."[63] St. John of the Cross wrote along the same lines:

> One does not reach this garden of full transformation which is the joy, delight and glory of spiritual marriage, without first passing through the spiritual espousal and the loyal and mutual love of betrothed persons. For, after the soul has been for some time the betrothed of the Son of God in gentle and complete love, God calls her and places her in His flowering garden to consummate this most joyful state of marriage with Him . . . Yet in this life this union cannot be perfect, although it is beyond words and thought.[64]

CHRISTIAN MARRIAGE: THE SACRAMENT

Pope John Paul II begins by analyzing Ephesians 5:21–33, what he calls the "crowning" of all of the passages of Scripture he considered when giving these talks.

> Be subject to one another out of reverence for Christ. Wives, be subject to your husbands, as to the Lord. For the husband is the head of the wife as Christ is the head of the church, his body, and is himself its Savior. As the church is subject to Christ, so let wives also be subject in everything to their husbands. Husbands,

---

[63] Quoted in M. F. Toal, *The Sunday Sermons of The Great Fathers*, *Vol. III* (San Francisco: Ignatius Press), 186.

[64] St. John of the Cross, "The Spiritual Canticle," in *The Collected Works of St. John of the Cross*, trans. Kieran Kavanaugh and Otilio Rodriguez (Washington, DC: ICS Publications, 1979), 497.

love your wives, as Christ loved the church and
gave himself up for her, that he might sanctify
her, having cleansed her by the washing of
water with the word, that he might present the
church to himself in splendor, without spot or
wrinkle or any such thing, that she might be
holy and without blemish. Even so husbands
should love their wives as their own bodies. He
who loves his wife loves himself. For no man
ever hates his own flesh, but nourishes and
cherishes it, as Christ does the church, because
we are members of his body. "For this reason a
man shall leave his father and mother and be
joined to his wife, and the two shall become
one flesh." This mystery is a profound one,
and I am saying that it refers to Christ and the
church; however, let each one of you love his
wife as himself, and the woman should have
reverence toward her husband.

John Paul II explains this passage is seen by the
Church as referring directly to the sacrament of matrimony. If a sacrament is "a visible sign of an invisible
reality," the body is that also, in a general sense. Vatican
II teaches that this passage from Ephesians "reveals—
in a particular way—*man to himself*, and makes *his
supreme vocation clear*."[65] The passage from Ephesians
brings together two key elements of the whole epistle:

The first is the mystery of Christ, which is
realized in the Church as an expression of the
divine plan for man's salvation; the second is
the Christian vocation as the model of life of
baptized persons and particular communities,
corresponding to the mystery of Christ or to
the divine plan for the salvation of man.[66]

---

[65] *Gaudium et Spes*, n. 22.
[66] John Paul II, *Man and Woman He Created Them*, 465, 468, 470–71.

In the opening words of the passage, "*Be subject to
one another out of reverence for Christ,*" the Holy Father
declares that the husband-wife relationship must
"spring from their common relationship with Christ,"
a "reverence for holiness." It is this that should bring
them to "be subject to one another."[67]

In saying, "As the Church is subject to Christ, so
let wives also be subject in everything to their husbands," the author of Ephesians is not saying that the
husband is to be the "master" of his wife, but that "it
is in her relationship with Christ . . . that the wife can
and should find the motivation for the relationship
with her husband." It is the mutual submission out
of reverence for Christ, however, that establishes the
strong foundation of the communion of persons in
marriage. The analogy in Ephesians 5 shows that marriage is truly Christian when the husband reflects the
love of Christ for the Church, and the wife reflects the
love that the Church gives back to Christ.[68]

By speaking of the husband as "head of the wife,"
and the wife as the "body of her husband," St. Paul is
suggesting they form "an organic union," while remaining two separate individuals. This is comparable to the
"one flesh" mentioned in Genesis.[69]

Ephesians speaks of the husband, in the image of
Christ, as the one who loves; the wife, in the image
of the Church, as the one who receives love. This
reception of love can be seen as the "submission" of
the wife to husband, as the Church submits to Christ.
And the union of the two is so close, that the spouse's
body is as one's own, and the husband is as occupied

---

[67] Ibid., 472–73.
[68] Ibid., 473–74, 476.
[69] Ibid., 479–80.

with the well-being of her body as that of his own. This is *agape*.[70]

The statement that the man nourishes his body as Christ does the Church can be seen as a reference to the Eucharist. It is with this, his own body, that *"Christ, in his spousal love, 'feeds' the Church."*[71]

St. Paul speaks indirectly, but fundamentally, "about the sacramentality of all Christian existence in the Church and especially about the sacramentality of marriage." The first of these concerns man's call to "holiness in Christ." The sacramentality of the Church is bound up with marriage, the oldest of the sacraments.[72]

The heart of the "mystery" in Ephesians is Jesus Christ. Those who accept the gift Christ brings can take part in the eternal mystery. Christ offers us the fruits of the redemption, and indeed, his very self, to us the Church, his spouse. This, of course, is in full continuity with the Old Testament themes of spousal love between God and his people, as found in Ezekiel 16, Hosea, Isaiah, and Song of Songs.[73]

The first aspect of God's love for his people mentioned in Ephesians is his fatherhood ("predestining us to be his adopted sons through Jesus Christ" [Eph 1:5]). The second is the spousal love of Christ for his Church, as we have seen. And this spousal love implies *"a participation in the divine nature"* (see 2 Pt 1:4). This makes clear the "radical character of grace" which divinizes us for this marriage.[74]

---

[70] Ibid., 485–86.
[71] Ibid., 486.
[72] Ibid., 488–89, 491.
[73] Ibid., 493–94.
[74] Ibid., 497, 501.

The Holy Father proposes that in original innocence, and in light of the spousal meaning of the body, man experiences himself as "a subject of holiness." This holiness, which he received in the beginning, is part of the "sacrament of creation." The words in Genesis 2:24, "the man . . . will unite with his wife and the two will become one flesh," given this holiness, "*constitute marriage as an integral part*, and in some sense the central part of the '*sacrament of creation*.'" Marriage is thus the "primordial sacrament." Marriage was intended not only to prolong creation but also to bestow the sacrament of creation, the "supernatural fruits," given from the beginning to all.[75]

Pope John Paul II suggests that marriage continues to be the stage for God's design, whereby the sacrament of creation approached mankind and made us ready for the sacrament of redemption. (Of course, the word *sacrament* is being used here in a more general way than that pertaining to the seven sacraments of the Church.) The mystery of redemption "hidden from all eternity in God" was symbolically manifested in the first marriage and is manifested "*in the indissoluble union of Christ with the Church*."[76]

Marriage, in a sense, is a "prototype" of the "new sacramental economy." Indeed, marriage is a prototype of all the sacraments of the New Covenant. This is because Christ gives spousal grace to the Church for all the sacraments. John Paul II points out that the description of marriage in Ephesians 5:22–33 is a "real renewal" of the saving reality of the first sacrament.[77]

The sacrament of marriage contains the seed of our

---

[75] Ibid., 506.
[76] Ibid., 507–9, 513.
[77] Ibid., 511–13.

final hope of life in the resurrection. It is not only something from the beginning, and a part of redeemed life, but also points to the hereafter.[78]

The Dimension of Sign

> When a husband and wife marry, they use a language of the body to form a communion of persons. This language of the body could be called a *"prophetism of the body"* insofar as it manifests the union of Christ and his Church. Man and wife, redeemed by Christ, exchange the language of the body, "reread in the truth." As the prophets said, the body speaks truth when it is faithful, and lies when it is unfaithful.[79]

Summary of Christian Marriage

In addressing the sacrament of marriage, JPII discusses Ephesians 5:21–33 to develop an understanding of marriage in Christ. It is their relationship with Christ that governs the spouses' relationship with each other—the husband loving, the wife receiving his love. In the "sacrament of creation" mankind knows himself to be a subject of holiness (in his innocence) and marriage is an essential manifestation of this sacrament. The mystery of redemption is made visible in marriage and in the love of Christ for the Church.

In other words, marriage in the Lord is to be a sign to the world of our union with God as part of Christ's Church. Living out the sacrament of salvation may involve a marital union with one's spouse here on earth, but most especially with God, our eternal spouse, whether we are married in this world or not.

---

[78] Ibid., 525.
[79] Ibid., 533, 535, 538.

LOVE AND FRUITFULNESS

At this point in his talks, John Paul II addresses the teaching of Pope Paul VI regarding marriage and procreation:

> The Church . . . *teaches* that each and every marriage act (*quilibit matrimonii usus*) must remain in itself open to the transmission of life. That teaching, often set forth by the magisterium, is founded upon the inseparable connection, willed by God and unable to be broken by man on his own initiative, between *the two meanings of the conjugal act*: the unitive [covenantal] meaning and the procreative [lifegiving] meaning.[80]

It is that "inseparable connection" which the pope considers here.[81]

Paul VI follows this passage with a sentence aimed at undergirding this teaching: "By its intimate structure, the conjugal act, while most closely uniting husband and wife, capacitates them for the generation of new lives according to laws inscribed in the very being of man and of woman."[82] Therefore, it can be said that the "*innermost structure*" (or "*nature*") of the conjugal act provides what is needed to see the two meanings that determine conjugal morality. The vision of these two and their inseparability is what was mentioned earlier, namely, "reading the 'language of the body' in truth."[83]

While John Paul II concedes that this teaching (inseparability) is not encountered in Scripture per se, but since it has been "often set forth by the

---

[80] *Humanae Vitae*, nn. 11–12.

[81] *Man and Woman*, 617–18.

[82] *Humanae Vitae*, n. 12.

[83] John Paul II, *Man and Woman*, 619–20.

magisterium."[84] "it follows that *this norm corresponds to revealed teaching as a whole* as contained in *the biblical sources.*"[85] The key here is more than the whole moral teaching of Scripture, but the "fuller whole" found in the "theology of the body" given earlier. As such, this teaching "is not only part of the natural law, but also of the *moral order revealed by God.*"[86]

The encyclical acknowledges that the domination of nature has progressed, but as JPII comments, it should not replace self-mastery. *Self-mastery* is constitutive of the human person and is natural. The use of artificial methods of birth control "breaks the constitutive dimension of the person, deprives man of the subjectivity proper to him and turns him into *an object of manipulation.*"[87]

The "language of the body" that spouses speak should convey the "*truth of the sacrament,*" the "whole truth of their persons." This truth includes both love and potential fruitfulness as meanings of the marriage act. Both are part of that truth; both are fulfilled together, and one might even say by way of one another. Thus, when stripped of its procreative power this act is no longer an act of love. The total reciprocal gift and total reciprocal acceptance which are part of the truth of this act, are missing. Acting against the very truth of conjugal communion—a core personal reality—is what makes contraception evil.[88]

The mutual submission mentioned in Ephesians 5:21 includes the continence or self-mastery needed to

---

[84] *Humanae Vitae*, n. 12.
[85] Ibid., n. 4.
[86] John Paul II, *Man and Woman*, 621.
[87] Ibid., 630–31.
[88] Ibid., 631–33.

honor the truth of the "*language of the body.*" Submit-
ting out of reverence for (or "fear of") Christ allows
us to consider it as a gift of the Holy Spirit, "fear of
the Lord." Chastity in marriage goes beyond simply
rejecting concupiscence of the flesh, to embracing
those meanings of "the language of the body" that
are foreign to concupiscence. It is these meanings that
enrich the spouses' interaction "by purifying, deepening and . . . simplifying it."[89]

Humanae Vitae acknowledged the conjugal act to
be a way of manifesting affection,[90] but it is, as JPII
says, a unique way which not only signifies personal
communion, but also has a life-giving power. Conjugal chastity not only preserves the "importance and
dignity" of the conjugal act regarding procreation, but
also its dignity, as it signifies the union of the spouses.
This latter point should awaken many other "manifestations of affection" to convey their "deep communion." Whereas some express fear that abstaining from
the marital act periodically could cause tensions, this
periodic abstinence rather provides an opportunity to
manifest affection in other ways, thereby enriching
marital communion. Sharing affection without the
marriage act can thus prepare for a more intimate
encounter when this act does take place.[91]

John Paul II identifies two types of attraction
between a man and woman, sensual and emotional.
The first is focused on the body; the second, on the person in his or her totality. Arousal inclines one toward
the marital act; emotion, toward the person. The latter
is often expressed by other "*manifestations of affection.*"

---

[89] Ibid., 645–46.
[90] *Humanae Vitae*, n. 16.
[91] John Paul II, *Man and Woman*, 647.

"Continence" according to Thomas Aquinas, and others before him, is more than just governing physical reactions to a person, but should "control and guide the whole sensual and emotive sphere of the human person." Continence should guide arousal toward a reasonable end, and emotion toward a selfless pursuit of the beloved.[92]

Periodic continence is a virtue, not as some biological method, but as part of the gift of one person to the other. This gift to the other is only possible when one has a self to give, a mature self that is under the control of one's own reason. A developed continence protects the spouses from concupiscence and fosters a "pure" (unselfish) communion of persons.[93]

The gifts of the Holy Spirit, and especially that of reverence, help spouses become deeply aware of the *"sign of the mystery of creation and redemption"* that their vocation contains. "Reverence for the two meanings of the conjugal act" must stem from a powerful awareness of the dignity of the spouse and the dignity of the new person they may bring forth. This reverence is a "salvific fear" of violating their vocation and all it symbolizes. This concerns the negative aspect of continence (rejecting concupiscence), and a high regard for both love and procreation.[94] To practice *"honorable regulation of fertility"* is part of the spirituality of marriage and family. The Spirit provides the gift of reverence, "reverence for God's work." This reverence helps couples maintain all that conjugal life should contain, including personal, ethical, and religious elements. The latter include "veneration for the majesty of the

---

[92] Ibid., 649–51.
[93] Ibid., 652.
[94] Ibid., 654.

Creator... and for spousal love of the Redeemer." This enlarges the field in which the mutual gift of husband and wife is played out, and the spousal meaning of each is fulfilled.[95]

Humanae Vitae can lead us to a framework of "conjugal spirituality." In this natural and supernatural environment an interior harmony is established between the "twofold meaning of the conjugal act."[96] In this way husband and wife live the truth of the "language of the body." According to the encyclical, this truth is tightly bound together with love.[97]

Summary of Love and Fruitfulness

The inseparability of the two meanings of the conjugal act is seen as part of its innermost structure and is discovered by "rereading the language of the body in truth."[98] When the procreative meaning is removed artificially, the reciprocal gift and acceptance are missing, thereby undermining the full meaning of love. Practicing periodic continence for valid reasons can open the couple to other displays of affection, which should deepen their communion and prepare them for a richer sexual encounter when that time comes. The gift of reverence, a "salvific fear," is what moves couples to honor their vocation and all it symbolizes, including love and procreation. To honor these things is to live the truth of the "language of the body."

To put it differently, contraception places a limit on the love between spouses, saying "I give you all of me except my fertility," and "I accept all of you

---

[95] Ibid., 655–56.
[96] *Humanae Vitae*, n. 12.
[97] John Paul II, *Man and Woman*, 657.
[98] Ibid., 619–20.

except your fertility." However, couples may practice periodic continence for valid reasons, and the marriage act carried out during the infertile times, when done in a spirit of openness, does not symbolize a love that is closed in on itself.

CONCLUSIONS

John Paul II's main goal in sharing these teachings was to establish the truth of a spousal meaning of the body, given at creation, wounded by original sin, restored by redemption, and fulfilled only in the life to come. Marriage and its bodily language are a symbol of the great mystery, fulfilled by Christ, spouse of the Church, in the redemption. To read the language of the body in truth includes realizing the inseparability of the two meanings of the conjugal act, both being part of the inner truth of the act. Contraception undermines both meanings, but periodic continence can enrich marital communion while honoring the full truth of marriage.

IVF Problems

THE EPOLITES' STORY IS NOT UNIQUE. Data for 2020 indicate that the success rate for in vitro fertilization with a woman under 35 was 55.1 percent live births per cycle.[1] For those women in Stephanie Epolite's age category (ages 38–40) the success rate for live births was under 26.4 percent per cycle.[2] Quite a gamble at $12,000–$30,000 per cycle!

How is IVF done? They often begin with giving drugs to women to increase the number of ova (eggs) produced in her body. Then several eggs are placed in a Petri dish and sperm is introduced into the dish as well. Once some of the eggs are fertilized, they are given a grade—for example, A, B, or C. Those graded C are simply discarded as if they were trash, and not human beings. Some of the As and Bs are frozen in suspended animation, alive but unable to grow. Then several A grade embryos are placed in the woman's womb. Only 3 percent of the ova fertilized will be born. That should cause great concern for anyone pursuing IVF who has moral convictions about the sanctity of human life.

---

[1] Mark Trolice, MD, "What is The Success Rate of IVF on the First Try?," The IVF Center, from a 2020 CDC Report, https://theivf-center.com/what-is-the-success-rate-of-ivf-on-the-first-try/#:~:-text=the%20first%20attempt%3F-,The%20average%20success%20rate%20of%20IVF%20on%20the%20first%20attempt,generally%20around%2020%2D35%25.

[2] Ibid.

THE CHURCH ON IVF

The *Catechism of the Catholic Church* condemns donor artificial insemination (involving sperm or ovum taken from someone other than the husband or wife) as violating the right of the child to be born of parents known to him within marriage.[3] Artificial techniques that involve only the couple are also morally unacceptable, because:

> They [separate] the sexual act from the procreative act. The act which brings the child into existence is no longer an act by which two persons give themselves to one another, but one that "entrusts the life and identity of the embryo into the power of doctors and biologists and establishes the domination of technology over the origin and destiny of the human person. Such a relationship of domination is in itself contrary to the dignity and equality that must be common to parents and children."[4]

> Under the moral aspect procreation is deprived of its proper perfection when it is not willed as the fruit of the conjugal act, that is to say, of the specific act of the spouses' union.... Only respect for the link between the meanings of the conjugal act and respect for the unity of the human being make possible procreation in conformity with the dignity of the person.[5]

The *Catechism* goes on to say:

---

[3] *Catechism of the Catholic Church*, para. 2376.
[4] Ibid., para. 2377. Quotation is from Congregation for the Doctrine of the Faith, *Donum Vitae*, 1987, II, 5.
[5] Congregation for the Doctrine of the Faith, *Donum Vitae*, 1987 II, 4. Quoted in *Catechism of the Catholic Church*, para. 2377.

A child is not something *owed* to one, but is a gift. The "supreme gift of marriage" is a human person. A child may not be considered a piece of property, an idea to which an alleged "right to a child" would lead. In this area, only the *child* possesses genuine rights: the right "to be the fruit of the specific act of the conjugal love of his parents," and "the right to be respected as a person from the moment of his conception.[6]

The Church points out that the very transferring of multiple embryos "implies a purely utilitarian treatment of embryos."[7]

---

[6] *Catechism of the Catholic Church*, para. 2378. Quotation from Congregation for the Doctrine of the Faith, *Donum Vitae*, 1987, II, 8.
[7] Congregation for the Doctrine of the Faith, *Dignitas Personae*, 2008, n. 15.

Wide-Ranging
NaPro Healings

I N JULY 2004, A NAPRO CONFERENCE
was held in Omaha, Nebraska, attended by over
400 physicians, pharmacists, medical practitioners,
and patients. Several patients told their own stories of
how NaPro had helped them.

One mother of eight was trying to homeschool her
children while dealing with debilitating depression.
She had already been treated successfully at the institute for repeated miscarriages. A nurse picked up on
her depression in a subsequent phone conversation.
She asked the woman to send in a blood sample, and
they discovered her hormone level to be one-third of
normal. With treatment, her depression disappeared.

A nineteen-year-old college student had such terrible
cramps during her menstrual period that for days each
month she was immobilized with pain. Doctors suggested either pain medication or the birth control pill.
The latter gave her slight relief. Her parents had heard
about Dr. Hilgers, and called the Institute. Following
a short period of charting, Hilgers discovered she had
endometriosis. She had surgery and vastly improved.

One mother suffered such postpartum depression
that she was beginning to feel as if having children
was a huge mistake. Her doctors told her this feeling
was normal and prescribed antidepressants. She con-
tacted Dr. Hilgers and he recognized this was way out
of line. He prescribed progesterone treatment, and her

heavy load was lifted. She quickly returned to her old, cheerful self.

One couple had had six heart-breaking miscarriages, and the wife was pessimistic that Dr. Hilgers could help. Her attitude was, "If God wants you to have children, he will give them to you." Dr. Hilgers commented, "If you have a clogged sink, are you just going to pray about it, or are you going to call a plumber?" He went to work with them, and two babies later they were beaming with joy, now firm believers in NaPro.[1]

HELPLESS IN NEW YORK?

One woman who was living in New York City went to a highly recommended OB/GYN (obstetrician/gynecologist) when she got engaged, to ask about possible fertility problems. She explained to him all her symptoms and wondered if he would explore the possibility of her having endometriosis. He didn't. He patted her on the back and walked her to the door, having prescribed some painkillers. She blurted out, "But I read [that] the only way this can be diagnosed is through laparoscopic surgery." (She was quite right.)[2]

"Surgery!" he blustered. "You don't need surgery." He said she was in good health and had no reason for any concern. Well, two and a half years into marriage and with no success at getting pregnant, Deborah was treated for Graves' disease. When that didn't solve her fertility, her OB/GYN started blindly looking for problems in her reproductive system. He suggested she should think about seeing an IVF specialist.[3]

---

[1] All these stories from Weber, "Agents of Change," op. cit.
[2] Jean Blair Packard, ed., *In Their Own Words, Women Healed* (Omaha: Pope Paul VI Institute, 2004), 63.
[3] Ibid., 61–62.

She had no use for artificial reproduction, so she went home and started researching other possibilities on the internet (smart woman). She found the Paul VI Institute, and called, hoping to get to see Dr. Hilgers. She was disappointed to learn that before seeing him she had to do two months of "NaPro tracking" in which she charted her monthly cycles, plus a month-long series of hormone tests before she could see him. Of course, she later came to appreciate this scientific approach to the problem, which is at the heart of the Creighton Model fertility program. She was able to do these things locally.[4]

By the time she got to Dr. Hilgers, he already had a strong suspicion that she had endometriosis. Plus, she had low levels of pre-ovulation estrogen. He did the laparoscopy[5] and discovered she did indeed have endometriosis, and he treated it with laser surgery during the laparoscopy (60 percent of cases can be treated during the initial laparoscopy). He also treated partial blockages in her fallopian tubes (which had been declared "clear and normal" in New York).[6] Also, by doing ultrasound tests during her two-week Omaha visit, they discovered that she had "premature follicle rupture."[7]

---

[4] Ibid., 62.

[5] "A *laparoscopy* is a type of minimally invasive surgery in which a small incision (cut) is made in the abdominal wall through which an instrument called a *laparoscope* is inserted to permit structures within the abdomen and pelvis to be seen. The abdominal cavity is distended and made visible by the instillation of absorbable gas, typically, carbon dioxide. A diversity of tubes can be pushed through the same incision in the skin. Probes or other instruments can thus be introduced through the same opening. In this way, a number of surgical procedures can be performed without the need for a large surgical incision." (From http://www.medterms. com/script/main/art.asp?articlekey=6211.)

[6] Packard, *In Their Own Words*, 63–64.

[7] Ibid., 64.

With all the data in, Dr. Hilgers recommended hormone treatment to deal with her low estrogen. She became pregnant within weeks of her treatment. Her baby, Olivia June Colloton, was born April 21, 2004. So much for her New York OB/GYN![8]

JUST THE FACTS

Some astonishing facts about NaPro:

1. It is more effective than IVF. Success rates are said to range from 40 percent to 60 percent vs. the IVF rate of about 30 percent per cycle.
2. It costs only a fraction of what IVF costs.
3. It is almost 80 percent effective in bringing about childbirth after several miscarriages.
4. It is 95 percent successful in treating pre-menstrual syndrome.
5. It is 95 percent successful in treating postpartum depression.
6. It cuts the rate of premature birth by almost 50 percent, thus lowering the frequency of birth-related injuries.
7. With NaPro, you can have more children after the first without paying the same large sum again.[9]

---

[8] Ibid., 65–66.
[9] Weber, "Agents of Change."

POSTSCRIPT

Thank you kindly for reading this book. Please, if it has helped you, or if you have suggestions for improvement, don't hesitate to email me at tgmorrow1@gmail.com. May God bless you on your journey.

BY THE SAME AUTHOR

Overcoming Sinful Anger: How to Master Your Emotions and Bring Peace to Your Life (Sophia Institute Press). Practical ways to conquer anger based on Sacred Scripture and the lives of the saints. At www.cfalive.com.

Overcoming Sinful Thoughts: How to Realign Your Thinking and Defeat Harmful Ideas (Sophia Institute Press). Getting rid of thoughts that distance us from God.
  "A masterpiece of solutions that points us to sainthood."
—Kevin Wells, author, *Priest & Beggar*

Christian Dating in a Godless World (Sophia Institute Press). The only guide for single Roman Catholics that covers it all, from where to find a good spouse to planning the wedding.

Straight to Heaven: A Catholic's Guide to the Spiritual Life (Sophia Institute Press). The shortest way to the Kingdom, using the lives and words of the saints.
  "What Saint Francis de Sales did for his generation, Fr. Morrow does for ours [in *Straight to Heaven*]." —Mike Aquilina

Achieving Chastity in an Unchaste World. A practical guide as to how to break free from addiction to lust and to find peace in the virtue of chastity—how not only to avoid sexual sins, including pornography, but also to do it joyfully. Preview it at www.cfalive.com.

Who's Who in Heaven: Real Saints for Families (Emmaus Road). 11 fascinating stories on saints that parents can read to their children. Lowest price at www.cfalive.com.

Fatima in Brief: A Treatment for All Ages (Catholic Faith Alive). A short (100 pp.) book on the Fatima apparitions with all the essentials, and without any fluff. Best price at www.cfalive.com.

Amazing Saints. Sts. Augustine, Margaret of Cortona, Teresa of Ávila, John Vianney, Damien the Leper, and Bl. Miguel Pro. Extraordinary lives! www.cfalive.com.

A Disciple's Way of The Cross. Stations of the Cross. Preview at www.cfalive.com.

World's Most Powerful Mysteries, revised edition with 20 Mysteries. Meditations in poetry and Sacred Scripture. Preview at www.cfalive.com.

Free rosary recording with Handel's *Messiah* in the background from our web site, www.cfalive.com. Click on rosary recording and follow instructions to download eight mp3 files to a phone or computer, or burn a CD.

For any of these books, other booklets, leaflets, and all the writings by the author, go to www.cfalive.com.

ABOUT THE AUTHOR

Rev. Thomas G. Morrow worked as an electrical engineer for twelve years before entering St. Charles Seminary in Philadelphia in 1977. He was ordained in 1982 for the Archdiocese of Washington, DC. He received a license in moral theology from the Dominican House of Studies in 1989, and a doctorate in sacred theology from the Pope John Paul II Institute for Studies on Marriage and Family in 1999. He has been the editor for the *Catholic Family Quarterly* for twenty-five years. He meets with various Catholic couples groups every month.